Contents

Chapter one

Introduction

1 | The purpose of these Revision Notes

This book is intended to help you succeed in your A-level or AS-level Sociology examination by:

- sharpening your focus on leading theories, concepts, methods, research studies, and debates

- reinforcing your knowledge of key sociological ideas

- pin-pointing any gaps in your sociological understanding

- providing a condensed survey of the sociological terrain

- reminding you why sociology is an exciting subject!

2 | Keep up good practice!

To maximise the benefit from these notes you need to follow *good practice* in your study of sociology. This involves:

- **Thinking sociologically about everyday life.** Relate ideas in books, articles and classroom discussion to your own experiences and develop a *sociological imagination*. This shows you how private concerns link up with public issues, how your own personal biography connects with history and how individuals can have an influence on society.

- **Reading up on sociology.** There are now many excellent introductory text books available and during your course of study you should aim to read some of these, as well as some original sociological studies. Note the strengths and weaknesses of the methodology used and refer to these in your examination / coursework. Look out for recent articles on the main topic areas covered in your syllabus (for example, in *Sociology Review*). Make use of dictionaries of sociology so you can define key terms and concepts clearly.

- **Using the mass media.** To do well in a sociology examination you will need to keep informed about current affairs and major issues of social and political debate. 'Quality' newspapers like *The Independent*, *The Guardian*, *The Daily Telegraph*, and *The Observer* regularly contain articles of sociological interest. Programmes of sociological interest are also often broadcast on radio and television. Sociological web-sites can be visited on the Internet. One of the great advantages of this subject is that it can be investigated anywhere, even in your armchair as you watch *Panorama* or *Newsnight*!

3 | Get on board!

Examination papers are set and assessed by specific examination boards. A wide range of topic options are now available, AS-level has been introduced, coursework (a personal sociological investigation) can be carried out, and it is also possible now to study the subject on a phased or 'modular' basis.

- Make sure you know which board you are sitting the examination with, what the syllabus is, and how you will be assessed.

3.1 Addresses of the Examining Boards

- The Associated Examining Board, Stag Hill House, Guildford, Surrey GU2 5XJ.

- *Copies of the Interboard Sociology Syllabus can be obtained from:*
  University of Oxford Delegacy of Local Examinations, Publications and Sales Department, Unit 23, Monks Brook Industrial Park, Chandlers Ford, Hampshire SO53 4RA.

- Northern Examinations and Assessment Board, Orbit House, Albert Street, Eccles, Manchester, M30 0WL.

4 | Sociology: The origins of the word

The word 'sociology' was coined by Auguste Comte 1839 and comes from the Latin *socius* (companion) and the Greek *ology* (study of). Thus, sociology is the study of social life / society.

4.1 Some definitions of sociology

'Sociology is a science which attempts the interpretative understanding of social action in order thereby to arrive at a causal explanation of its course and effects.' (M.Weber).

'Sociology may be defined as the study of society, that is, of the web or tissue of human interactions and human inter-relationships.' (M.Ginsberg).

'Sociology was the first science to be concerned with social life as a whole, with the whole complex of institutions and social groups which constitutes a society. The fundamental conception, or directing idea, in sociology is that of *social structure*.' (T.B. Bottomore).

'Sociology is a scientific mode of analysing social relationships.' (P. Worsley).

'Sociology is the study of human social life, groups and societies.' (A. Giddens).

'... sociology is concerned with the problem of society, and society is something formed by oneself and other people together; the person who studies and thinks about society is himself a member of it.' (N. Elias).

5 | Further reading

Barnard, A. and Burgess, T. (1996) *Sociology Explained*, Cambridge, Cambridge University Press.

Bilton, T. *et al.* (1996) *Introductory Sociology*, Basingstoke, Macmillan.

Giddens, A. (1997) *Sociology*, 3rd edition, (1997) Cambridge, Polity Press.

Jorgensen, N. *et al.* (1997) *Sociology: An Interactive Approach*, London, HarperCollins.

Kirby, M. *et al* (1997) *Sociology In Perspective*, Oxford, Heinemann.

Macionis, J. and Plummer, K. (1998) *Sociology. A Global Introduction*, Englewood Cliffs, N. J. Prentice-Hall.

Marsh, I. *et al.* (1996) *Making Sense of Society. An Introduction to Sociology*, London, Longman.

O'Donnell, M. (1997) *A New Introduction to Sociology*, 4th edition, Walton on Thames, Thomas Nelson.

Taylor, P. *et al.* (1996) *Sociology In Focus*, Ormskirk, Causeway Press.

Dictionaries of Sociology

Jary, D. and Jary, J. (1995) *Collins Dictionary of Sociology*, Glasgow, HarperCollins.

Lawson, T. and Garrod, J. (1996) *The Complete A–Z Sociology Handbook*, London, Hodder and Stoughton.

Marshall, G. (ed.) (1994) *The Concise Oxford Dictionary of Sociology*, Oxford, Oxford University Press.

5.1 Help with coursework

Langley, P. and Corrigan, P. (1993) *Managing Sociology Coursework*, Lewes, Connect.

5.2 Periodicals and annual publications

Sociology Review (published four times a year) is available from: Subscriptions Department, Philip Allan Publishers, Market Place, Deddington, Oxfordshire, OX15 0SE.

Another highly informative publication (produced annually) is: *Sociology Update*, 32 Shirley Road, Leicester, LE2 3TL.

The Social Science Teacher is published three times a year by the Association for the Teaching of the Social Sciences, P. O. Box 61, Watford, WD2 2NH.

Each year HMSO publishes *Social Trends*. This contains statistical information on changing patterns of life in Britain and is available in reference libraries.

Chapter two

The sociological approach: theorists, concepts, perspectives

'The fundamental ideas of European sociology are best understood as responses to the problem of order created at the beginning of the nineteenth century by the collapse of the old regime under the blows of industrialism and revolutionary democracy"

Robert Nisbet, *The Sociological Tradition*, (1970).

1 Classic theorists

1.1 The key ideas of Karl Marx (1818–83)

- **Class conflict** In capitalist society there are two antagonistic classes: the **bourgeoisie** (which owns the means of production such as factories) and the **proletariat** (or working class) which has to sell its labour power in order to survive.

- **Base and superstructure** The economic structure of society (the 'base') can be pictured as 'supporting' the social and political structure of society (the 'superstructure').

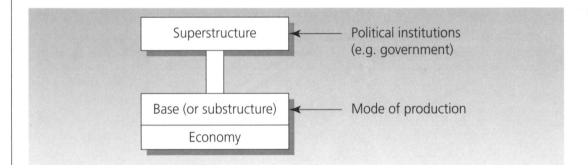

- **Epochs of history** In tribal society (or primitive communism) the surplus of wealth was too small to fight over. In ancient societies (e.g. Greece and Rome) a class struggle over control of surplus wealth was waged between slave owners and slaves. In feudal society the struggle was between landowners and peasants, and in capitalist society between the owners of capital and the proletarians.

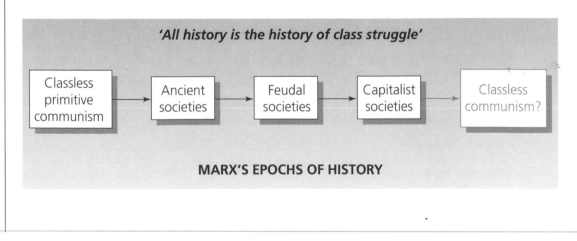

MARX'S EPOCHS OF HISTORY

- **Alienation** Work in a capitalist society is merely a means to an end, an instrumental way of gaining money. It does not fulfil an individual's creative needs. Consequently the worker experiences a loss of self and feels powerless and dehumanised.

- **Dialectical method** This was influenced by the philosophy of Hegel. **Capitalists** (thesis) and **workers** (antithesis) struggle against each other and this conflict leads to the formation of a **new classless society** in which there are neither capitalists or workers (synthesis). Marx believed that capitalist society would be transformed by revolutionary change.

For Marx conflict is the motor of social change.

1.2 The key ideas of Emile Durkheim (1858–1917)

- **Social facts** Social facts are external forces which pressure individuals to act in particular ways. Society is a 'conscious being ... with its own special nature, distinct from that of its members, and a personality of its own different from individual personalities.'

- **Social solidarity** In traditional agricultural societies the bonds which hold people together are based on **mechanical** solidarity: individuals share the same beliefs and values. In modern industrial societies the bonds which hold people together are based on **organic** solidarity: individuals do not share the same collective sentiments but are economically inter-dependent on each other.

- **Anomie** The word comes from the Greek origin *anomia* (absence of law) and refers to the lack of a stable framework of meaning and guidelines in individuals' lives. Durkheim saw modern industrial societies as highly individualistic and lacking social solidarity. Intermediate groups (e.g. based on occupation, on the local community, etc.) had to be strengthened if anomic trends were to be checked.

- **The sacred and the profane** The world is divided into two domains: the **sacred** (religious life) and the **profane** (ordinary everyday life). A key function of religion is to 'strengthen the bonds attaching the individual to the society of which he is a member.'

Durkheimians assign primacy to society over the individual.

1.3 The key ideas of Max Weber (1864–1920)

- **Interpretative sociology** Sociology studies the subjective meanings which underpin behaviour. The concept of **Verstehen** (understanding) refers to a process of psychological sympathy: the investigator 'feels himself into' the state of mind of the individual. Weber distinguished between two types of motivated actions: **zweckrational** (means to an end, 'getting from A to B' rationality) and **wertrational** (the pursuit of absolute ends, the actions of 'true believers' who will die for a cause).

- **Role of ideas in history** Weber is critical of the materialist view that social change is only caused by economic factors and believes that ideas can change the direction of the locomotive of history. Islam, the Crusades, and Protestantism are all examples of ideas that have produced social change as is Marxism – the very theory which rejected the idealist view that ideas can change history.

- **Three dimensions of stratification**

  - *Class:* based on a shared 'market situation' – the same 'typical chance for a supply of goods, external living conditions, and personal life experiences...'

  - *Status:* based on prestige and lifestyle. Status groups are stratified in terms of consumption, and their members feel they belong together and form a community

  - *Power:* based on the capacity to impose one's will on others (e.g. political parties to gain control of the state and / or using pressure groups to influence the policies of government).

Weberians seek to understand the meaning of behaviour.

- **Forms of authority** Authority depends upon consent: individuals obey because they believe it is right (legitimate) to do so.

  - *Charismatic:* legitimacy (the system of consent) rests on a belief in the exceptional qualities of an individual

  - *Traditional:* legitimacy rests on a belief in the sanctity of immemorial tradition. It has 'always existed'

  - *Rational-legal:* legitimacy rests on a belief in the legality of a consciously created order. Weber believed that bureaucracy will increase. A spirit of rationalisation (the application of rational calculation) will eventually pervade every aspect of life and produce a widespread sense of the 'disenchantment of the world'.

1.4 The key ideas of Herbert Spencer (1820–1903)

- **The organismic analogy** Spencer compared society to an organism or living creature which has 'organs' or 'internal arrangements' for the transportation of food and the removal of sewage.

- **The functional inter-dependence of social units** 'Twisting off the head of a fowl is fatal. Not even a reptile...can live when its body is divided... (similarly) Middlesex separated from its surroundings would in a few days have all its social processes stopped by lack of supplies.' In studying society one must examine its anatomy – its structure – and the functions of the component units.

- **Evolution of society** By evolution Spencer meant both increased differentiation (or specialisation) and integration (co-ordination of the various specialist parts). As a society becomes more 'developed' so its social structure becomes more complex.

Spencer analyses society in terms of structure and functions.

1.5 The key ideas of Georg Simmel (1858–1918)

- **Social interaction** Society 'is merely the name for a number of individuals connected by interaction.'

- **The individual within society and outside it** 'Man is both social link and being for himself'. The individual is acted upon and self-actuating.

- **Interaction in terms of reciprocal relationships** 'In so far as man is a social being, to each of his obligations there corresponds a right on the part of others... since every person with obligations in one way or another also possesses rights, a network of rights and obligations is thus formed.'

- **The positive function of conflict** Conflict acts as a safety valve for negative feelings and can strengthen bonds within social groups. Society is 'sewn together' by criss-crossing conflicts.

- **View of urban life** '...one never feels as lonely and as deserted as in this metropolitan crush of persons.' Urban life is characterised by physical proximity and social distance, mutual reserve, and a blasé outlook.

Simmel is one of Sociology's neglected classic theorists.

1.6 The key ideas of Ferdinand Tonnies (1855–1936)

- **The ideal-type distinction between *Gemeinschaft* and *Gesellschaft*** Gemeinschaft (community) relationships are close and intimate and are found in small-scale (e.g. rural) societies. Gesellschaft (association) relationships are more superficial and impersonal and are found in large-scale (e.g. urban-industrial) societies. However, critics of the Gemeinschaft / Gesellschaft distinction point out that rural 'communities' are sharply divided by class and that close-knit working-class communities exist in 'impersonal' urban areas.

The two German words all sociologists know!

- **The growth of urban-industrialism** This made a dramatic impact on social relationships. For Shelley 'Hell is a city just like London.' Engels in 1844 wrote of 'The brutal indifference, the unfeeling isolation of each in his private interest...' Tonnies' influence is evident in *Urbanism As A Way of Life* (1938) by Louis Wirth which put forward the view that there were two 'basic models of human association in contemporary civilisation': rural-agricultural and urban-industrial. The urban way of life involves: 'the substitution of secondary for primary contacts, the weakening of bonds of kinship, and the declining significance of the family.'

2 | Conflict or consensus: the broad theoretical perspectives

'In sociology there has been a tendency for theorists to take one side or the other, to see society as being better characterised and described primarily in terms of clashing interests or in terms of shared agreements', E.C. Cuff, W.W. Sharrock, and D.W. Francis, *Perspectives In Sociology* (1990).

- **Structural-consensus theory:** individual behaviour is shaped by society, and shared cultural values bind the members of a society together.

- **Structural-conflict theory:** individual behaviour is shaped by society, but conflicts of interests and values create deep social divisions.

- **Action theory:** individuals interact with other people, interpret other people's behaviour, and express meaning and intention through their actions.

2.1 Structural-consensus theory

- Acceptance of shared cultural norms and values is a key theme of consensus theory. Individual behaviour is channelled and pushed into particular directions.

- **Functionalism** is an example of this perspective. It was influenced by anthropologists like A.R. Radcliffe-Brown (1881–1955) and Bronislaw Malinowski (1884–1942). Their investigations of small-scale non-industrial societies led them to conclude that social institutions (e.g. the family, work, and religion) formed part of an inter-dependent system.

- Some functionalists have compared society to a living creature (the **'organismic'** or **'biological' analogy**) or to a machine (e.g. open the back of a clock and look at the inter-dependent parts of this complex mechanism).

- According to Talcott Parsons (1902–79) – the uncrowned 'king' of functionalism – if a social system is to survive over time a number of vital tasks have to be performed which can be summed up in the acronym GAIL: 1) **G**oal-attainment: goals are set by the political sub-system, 2) **A**daptation: mobilising resources through the economic sub-system; 3) **I**ntegration: regulating tensions through the conflict-resolution sub-system; 4) **L**atency (or pattern maintenance): the socialisation sub-system transmits cultural values from one generation to another.

Criticisms of structural-consensus theory are that:

- If individuals are socialised into sharing common values why do riots, protest marches, and sometimes even revolutions occur? If society is characterised by stability and harmony what causes social change to take place?

- It is a mistake to 'reify' society and analyse it as if it was a living organism or 'thing'. A society is composed of 'knowledgeable agents' – conscious, thinking, individuals – not inanimate objects or biological organs.

- Consensus theory represents a form of conservative ideology and is designed to provide a justification for the status quo.

Parsonian functionalism dominated Sociology until the late 1960s.

Can consensus theory explain conflict?

2.2 Structural-conflict theory

- A key theme of conflict theory is that societies are made up of 'unequally advantaged groups' which have different interests.

- Division, inequality and conflict (not consensus, co-operation and agreement) are central features of society. **Marxism** is a leading example of this approach. The class which owns and controls the means of production also controls the state. Members of the economically dominant class staff the upper reaches of the state apparatus (the civil service, judiciary, military, etc.). Business interests apply pressure on government to ensure that policies which are favourable to their interests are implemented.

- **Weberians** also see society as characterised by a struggle between social groups for control over, and access to, scarce and valued resources. The focus of conflict is not confined to wealth and income but includes power and status.

Criticisms of structural-conflict theory are that:

- If value-consensus is a cultural myth manufactured by powerful groups, and if society is in fact deeply divided by inequality and conflict, how is social stability to be explained?

- If class divisions are as entrenched as Marxists claim, and if the values of the dominant class are radically different from those of the working class, why have industrial societies like Britain not experienced a revolution?

- Social action theorists argue that it is the choices and decisions of individuals – not the mere existence of structural divisions – which determine whether or not conflict takes place.

Can conflict theory explain consensus?

2.3 Action theory

- In contrast to a 'society makes man' perspective a number of sociologists have put forward a 'man makes society' perspective. Action or interpretative theory rejects any suggestion that individuals are 'puppets' who are pushed this way and that by external structures. Individuals have the capacity to 'work out what is going on around them, and then to choose to act in a particular way, in the light of this interpretation' – P. Jones, *Studying Society* (1993).

- **G. H. Mead (1863–1931) and the Symbolic Interactionists** Mead argued that the self is made up of two elements: the **I**, which is a person's private inner self, and the **Me**, which is the public outer self. Identities are formed in a process of communication with others and the role of **significant others** (such as parents) is especially influential. People try to imagine how others see them. Each person they meet acts as a looking glass and reflects back an image of their own self.

- **Erving Goffman (1922–82) and Dramaturgy** In *Presentation of Self in Everyday Life* (1959) Goffman views social life from a theatrical (or **dramaturgical**) perspective. Social reality is 'created' by individuals who 'act out' certain parts and try to engineer favourable impressions. Drama, a concern for appearances, a fear of being 'caught out' – these are enduring realities of the human condition. We are all actors who are afraid that we might forget our lines.

- **Harold Garfinkel (1917–) and Ethnomethodology** Garfinkel criticised conventional sociology for its failure to study 'how society gets put together.' The focus of ethnomethodology (the most 'micro' branch of 'micro' sociology) is on common-sense 'folk' knowledge which makes 'everyday rationality' and ordinary social life possible.

- **Alfred Schutz (1899–1959) and Phenomenology** The phenomena of the world – everything and everybody in it – are experienced through our senses. Schutz argued that the aim of sociology is to understand the 'life-worlds' of individuals, to 'prise open' their consciousness and common-sense perspectives.

Action theory rejects Structuralism.

Criticisms of action theory are that:

Can social
structures be
ignored?

- It fails to sufficiently acknowledge the degree to which individuals' lives are shaped by events and forces outside their personal control.

- It is an illusion to see people as free-floating and autonomous actors who are in complete charge of the scripts of their own lives.

- Ethnomethodologists are preoccupied with trivial aspects of behaviour. (Studies have been made of how people walk along the pavement and of how individuals manage the first five seconds of a conversation.)

3 | Specific perspectives

3.1 Mertonian functionalism

- Robert Merton (1910–) makes a distinction between **manifest** functions (which are recognised and intended) and **latent** functions (which are not recognised and intended). For example:

- On a manifest level X goes to a football match to support Bristol Rovers. However Mertonians see X's football supporting as being *really* (or latently) about strengthening social integration in an anomic urban culture.

- On a manifest level Y takes hard drugs in order to pursue escapist pleasure. However, Y is unemployed and feels 'superfluous' to the economy. The objective logic of the social system overrides the motives and intentions of individuals, and the latent function of the drug sub-culture is to reduce the life-expectancy of members of marginal groups.

3.2 Neo-functionalism

Neo: one of
Sociology's
favourite prefixes!

- *Neo* simply means 'new', 'modern', or 'revived'. It is applied to theoretical approaches which have been developed and refined by later thinkers.

- Neo-functionalists such as Kingsley Davis reject the view that classic functionalist concepts (such as socialisation, norms, culture and consensus) can be bolted together into a single and all-encompassing theoretical system. What they see as valuable in functionalism is its method of analysis and the view of society as comprising a system of interacting parts.

- Critics like E.C. Cuff *et al.* believe that Davis's approach eliminates 'that which is actually distinctive about functionalism, which is the analysis of the interaction of system parts *relative to a notion of system needs*'.

3.3 Neo-Marxist conflict theory

Marx believed that the class contradictions inherent in capitalist society would lead to revolution. However, although a communist party took power in the economically under-developed society of Russia, in advanced capitalist societies such as Britain revolution has failed to occur. Twentieth-century neo-Marxists have attempted to explain why the revolution in the West was blocked / delayed / indefinitely postponed.

- **V.I. Lenin (1870–1924).** One of the leading organisers of the 1917 Russian Revolution, Lenin believed a revolution would not happen 'automatically'. Left to itself the working class would accept its lot. Only by creating an organisation of professional revolutionaries and injecting Marxist ideology into the proletariat could capitalism be overthrown. Lenin believed that the working class in Britain (a country which at that time controlled a vast empire) had been 'bribed' into voting for pro-capitalist parties by the profits extracted from the exploitation of less-developed countries.

Marx's response to some Neo-Marxism was to declare: 'I am not a Marxist!'

- **Antonio Gramsci (1891–1937).** The author of the 'Prison Notebooks' was imprisoned by Mussolini from 1926 until his death. He believed that the dominant class had persuaded the masses that capitalism – not socialism – was 'common sense'. He developed the concept of **hegemony** – the cultural leadership exercised by one class over another (from the Greek *hegemon* meaning leader or ruler). Hegemony describes a situation in which a certain way of life and thought prevails and where one view of reality is diffused throughout society's institutions and people's private lives.

- **L. Althusser (1918–90).** The **ideological state apparatus** (institutions like schools, churches, the media, as well as the family) indoctrinate the mass of the population with the dominant ideology and thereby engineer consent for the status quo. If persuasion and indoctrination fail then the **repressive state apparatus** (army, police etc.) will be mobilised to keep the working class in line.

- **Critical theory and the Frankfurt School.** The Frankfurt Institute for Social Research was founded in 1922. Leading theorists included Max Horkheimer, Theodor Adorno, and Herbert Marcuse. They accepted Marx's 'critical' analysis of capitalism, but were also 'critical' of the working class. They believed it had lost its revolutionary potential and had been absorbed into the existing social order by consumerism and the mass media. Affluent proletarians spend their time watching television and storming the shopping malls instead of storming the barricades!

3.4 Elitist conflict theory

Some Non-Marxists also believe in the class struggle.

- **Vilfredo Pareto (1848–1923) and Gaetano Mosca (1858–1941).** In all societies 'two classes of people appear – a class that rules and a class that is ruled' (Mosca). This division between a powerful and well-organised élite and a disorganised and apathetic mass is – contrary to the utopian hopes of Marxist revolutionaries – inevitable. A 'circulation of élites' (Pareto) ensures that talented members of the masses are promoted into the élite and mediocre members of the élite are relegated into the masses. All that revolutions mean is that the masses will be exploited by a new élite instead of the old one.

- **Ralf Dahrendorf (1928–).** The Marxist illusion was to believe that the abolition of private ownership would result in the abolition of conflict. In reality 'control over the means of production is but a special case of authority...' Today we live in a 'post-capitalist society' in which the middle class has expanded, social mobility increased, and managers – not owners of the means of production – hold the levers of power.

3.5 Structuration theory

Can society both make and be made by individuals?

- Anthony Giddens (1938–) has attempted to resolve the 'society makes man' versus 'man makes society' ('Structure' versus 'Agency') debate. A key concept is **duality of structure**: the social structure is both 'the medium and outcome' of social action. Structures are 'forms of enablement' which make it possible for individuals to achieve their goals. Individuals are **knowledgeable agents** and not 'cultural dopes'. While structures constrain individuals, individuals can also shape structures, use structures for their own purposes, and bring about changes in structures.

- Critics see structuration theory as understating the degree to which structures thwart and impede individual goals, especially those of powerless individuals. Inmates of concentration camps in Nazi-occupied Europe in the 1940s would have found it hard to believe that the social structures which constrained them were also 'forms of enablement.'

3.6 Post-modernism

Are we living in a new period of history?

- Dramatic changes have taken place since the 1960s. In the view of Jean Baudrillard (1929–) in today's media-saturated consumer world it is no longer possible to distinguish artificial simulations of reality from reality itself. The 'real' has merged with 'representations' of the 'real'. 'Everything becomes undecidable', including – so critics argue – the question of whether post-modernism itself is a 'real' theory or a simulacrum of a theory (a theory which has no referent to any reality other than itself!).

- 'We have discovered that nothing can be known with any certainty, since all pre-existing 'foundations' of epistemology (knowledge) have been shown to be unreliable' – Anthony Giddens – *The Consequences of Modernity* (1990).

- The post-modernist Jean-Francois Lyotard (1924) believes that all attempts at providing total explanations of the nature of society and history, of formulating *metanarratives* (grand 'stories' or theories, such as Marxism) have failed. Moreover, they deserve to fail. In Lyotard's view all theories which claim to have discovered 'truths' and 'certainties' lead ultimately to domination and tyranny.

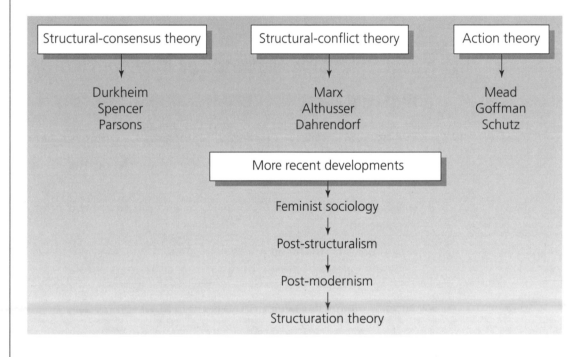

Structural-consensus theory	Structural-conflict theory	Action theory
Durkheim Spencer Parsons	Marx Althusser Dahrendorf	Mead Goffman Schutz

More recent developments

↓

Feminist sociology

↓

Post-structuralism

↓

Post-modernism

↓

Structuration theory

4 | Checklist of key terms and concepts

Bourgeoisie and Proletariat   Alienation   Social facts   Mechanical and Organic solidarity   Anomie   Modernity   *Verstehen*   Value-relevance   Power and Authority   Charismatic, Traditional, and Rational-legal authority   Rationalisation   The Organismic Analogy   Macro and Micro   GAIL   Manifest and Latent   Neo Hegemony   Ideological state apparatus and repressive state apparatus   Duality of structure   MetaNarrative   Simulacra

5 | Further reading

Cuff, E.C. Sharrock, W.W. and Francis, D.W. (1990) *Perspectives in Sociology*, London, Routledge.

Haralambos, M. and Holborn, M. (1995) *Sociology: Themes and Perspectives*, London, HarperCollins.

Jones, P. (1993) *Studying Society: Sociological Theories and Research Practices*, London, Collins Educational.

The sociological approach: methods

1 | Positivism

- *Auguste Comte* (1798–1857) believed that sociology would play a key role in shaping the new industrial order. It would be based on **positivism** – i.e., on the facts of experience.

- Positivists see science as establishing the truth through empirical investigation, systematic observation, and logical analysis. The classic example of positivist methodology is the laboratory experiment. It delivers objective knowledge – knowledge which does not differ according to who discovers it.

- Positivists argue that sociology should concern itself simply with the 'facts', not with moral judgements – describing what 'is', not what 'ought to be'.

2 | The Scientific Method (or hypothetico-deductive method)

- **Observations** are made of the phenomena being investigated.

- Theoretical knowledge is used to formulate a **hypothesis** – an untested explanation of causation.

- Systematic observation is carried out and **empirical data** (factual information) collected.

- The **data is analysed** in order to see whether the hypothesis is supported or refuted by the evidence, proved or disproved, confirmed or falsified.

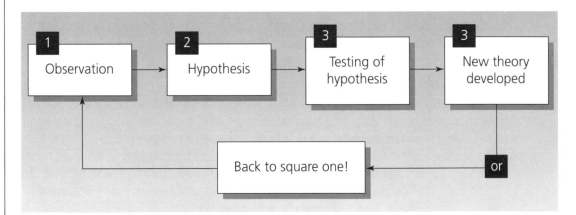

2.1 Testing theories: falsification and confirmation

- The **Principle of Falsification** was put forward by Karl Popper (1902–94) in 1959. The hallmark of a scientific statement is that it can be empirically tested (i.e. by experience and with our senses). An unscientific statement – such as 'God is in heaven' – cannot be empirically tested.

- In Popper's view scientific knowledge is advanced by making conjectures (theories) and bold guesses which are then systematically tested. Only if a theory is not *falsified* is it accepted – and then only provisionally because it could be disproved tomorrow.

- Once a hypothesis has been formulated the scientist then tries to assess its *validity* by testing it against the empirical evidence. His aim is either to confirm or to falsify it – by collecting as much evidence as possible in its favour or by trying to disprove it.

2.2 Public knowledge

- In 1968 J. M. Ziman described science as a form of 'Public Knowledge' because it doesn't just involve empirical investigation and a logical methodology. New theories and research findings also have to be published, placed in the public domain, and subjected to rigorous scrutiny by other scientists.

2.3 How 'scientific' is the scientific method?

Critics of the positivist view of science point out that:

Theories in both the natural science and social science rest on paradigms.

- Scientific knowledge rests on accepted values and perceptions, not on pure evidence alone. Scientists have a model of reality – a **paradigm** – which is based upon a set of shared assumptions. Astronomy was once dominated by a 'the sun revolves around the earth' paradigm. Evidence then emerged which suggested this should be replaced by a 'the earth revolves around the sun' paradigm. Eventually a paradigm revolution took place and what was once seen as 'abnormal science' came to be regarded as 'normal science.'

- The underlying forms of the social and natural world cannot be 'unmasked' by positivist-style empirical investigation alone. This view is known as Realism, and has been summarised as 'the belief that there are real structures of society which exist, but which are not necessarily open to observation. The implication of this is that the pure empiricist position, which is to go out and collect facts and to consider only these as scientific, must be rejected as presenting an incomplete view of the world: it cannot account for the fundamental structures of society,' – M. Kirby *et al.* – *Sociology In Perspective* (1997).

- The reality of scientific research is far messier than positivists suggest. Many scientific discoveries have come about by chance, inspired guesswork, and sheer fluke. Scientists' descriptions of how they have carried out their research has occasionally been 'economical with the truth'. The prospect of securing lucrative contracts from business or government can tempt some scientists into 'massaging' and misrepresenting their findings.

- Patrick McNeil points out that the word ' "Data" means, literally, "things that are given" ', and assumes a positivist world view. 'But if knowledge is created and constructed, then "data" is not "given", but produced.' *Research Methods* (1985).

2.4 How 'scientific' is sociology?

Sociology forms part of the science of culture. Physics forms part of the science of nature.

- Anthony Giddens defines science as the use of *'systematic methods of empirical investigation, the analysis of data, theoretical thinking and the logical assessment of arguments* to develop a body of knowledge about a particular subject-matter. According to this definition, sociology is a scientific endeavour' – *Sociology* (1997).

- The subject matter of sociology – human meaning – is quite different from the subject matter of the natural sciences. The elements studied in chemistry or physics do not possess consciousness. Special problems are involved in studying people rather than things, and consequently a 'science of culture' requires a different methodology from a 'science of nature.'

- In the view of Max Weber sociology must seek to understand (*verstehen*) the subjective dimension of action, the state of mind of individuals. Sociology cannot live by positivist methods alone.

3 | Values and Sociology

Anti-positivists reject the view that Sociology can be value-free.

- Sociologists are members of society and their own emotions and values will influence the research they carry out. In his 1944 study of the position of black people in the USA Gunnar Myrdal argued that it is impossible to be neutral about racism. One best serves the pursuit of scientific objectivity by making one's personal values explicit so that readers can clearly see where the biases are.

- Values influence the choice of what is to be studied and thus the 'horse of bias' has bolted even before any research has been carried out. Weber refers to this as **value-relevance**.

- Value-judgements cannot be avoided since all research has moral consequences. Deciding not to make a value-judgement is itself a value-judgement.

Whose side are you on – Becker's or Gouldner's?

- In 1970 Howard Becker claimed that sociologists are faced with a clear ethical choice when conducting research – that of identifying with powerful groups in society and thus accepting the frame of reference of the privileged, or identifying with the powerless and directing their research to improving the lot of the underdog. However, in 1973 Alvin Gouldner challenged Becker's view. 'Isn't it good for a sociologist to take the standpoint of someone outside of those most immediately engaged in a specific conflict, or outside of the group being investigated? Isn't it precisely this outside standpoint, or our ability to adopt it, which is the one source and one possible meaning of sociological objectivity?'.

4 | Research methods

4.1 Quantitative and qualitative methods

Positivists favour quantitative methods of investigation and anti-positivists favour qualitative methods.

- **Quantitative** research focuses on measurement and the collection of numerical data (statistics and 'number crunching').

- **Qualitative** research focuses on interpreting meaning and feelings and is expressed in words rather than numbers.

4.2 Types of data

- **Primary data** is collected first-hand by the sociologist.

- **Secondary data** is second-hand – it is material which already exists – (e.g. official statistics, newspaper articles, diaries, autobiographies, letters, historical documents).

4.3 Sampling

- When a **census** of the population is carried out information is collected from every household. Other **social surveys** are based on smaller samples of the population.

- When examining research findings one should always check the size of the sample (the **sample fraction**). Valid generalisations cannot be drawn from very small and unrepresentative samples. An early example of the hazards of sampling was the 1936 opinion poll organised by the *Literary Digest* magazine in New York. A poll of readers' voting intentions suggested that the Democratic candidate for the Presidential election would lose – but he won comfortably. The middle-class readers of the magazine polled by the 'Digest' were untypical of the general population.

Examples of sampling techniques

- **Random sampling:** based on pure chance. Everyone has the same likelihood of being selected.

- **Systematic (or quasi-random) sampling:** every nth person in the sampling frame is chosen. A **sampling frame** is the list from which those to be sampled are drawn (such as an electoral register).

- **Stratified sampling:** a random sample is taken from pre-determined categories such as occupation, age, gender, or ethnicity. This increases the chances of obtaining a representative sample.

- **Quota sampling:** the 'High Street' version of stratified sampling. The researcher stands in a city centre street and interviews quotas of people (e.g. n number of single men, women aged over 30, manual workers, etc.). This is a quick but less reliable method.

- **Cluster or multi-stage sampling:** instead of researchers interviewing respondents in every city a number of representative cities are selected. Then a number of representative areas are selected within each of the selected cities. Thus one sample is drawn from another.

Samples can be unrepresentative yet still produce valuable results. Examples include:

- **Snowball sampling:** this is based on personal recommendation and is sometimes referred to as opportunity sampling. The researcher finds one suitable respondent, who then introduces the researcher to another suitable respondent, who in turn introduces the researcher to another and so on. It provides a way of investigating groups which may be reluctant to be investigated.

- **Purposive sampling:** those selected are of particular relevance to the investigation. A classic example is the *Affluent Worker* study (1968) in Luton. The above-average wages of the Luton car workers made them untypical of the British working class. But this very untypicality made them an ideal group on which to test out the embourgeoisement theory.

4.4 Observational methods

- **Non-participant covert observation:** e.g. observing a group through a one-way screen, or filming them.

- **Covert participant observation** This is an example of qualitative research and is sometimes referred to as 'ethnographic' research – describing the way of life of a group or society. The investigator becomes a participating member of a group but does not inform anyone of her/his true purpose. *Black Like Me* (1962) by John Griffin is an example of this approach. Griffin (a white journalist who was not an academic sociologist) had himself injected with a preparation which changed the colour of his skin. He then lived for a month as a black person in several towns in the southern USA, and gained new insight and understanding into the nature of racism.

- **Overt participant observation** The investigator becomes a participating member of a group but does inform people of her/his purpose. Unlike covert participant observation the privacy of those being studied is respected, no deception takes place, and informed consent is given. However some groups might refuse to consent to being studied, and a researcher could be faced with the choice of either unethically deceiving them or of unethically abandoning research which s/he feels a moral obligation to pursue.

> Different investigations require different types of sample.

> Participant observation is a form of ethnographic research.

4.5 Strengths and weaknesses of research techniques

- **Questionnaires** are lists of questions designed to gain information on attitudes and behaviour. They can be **closed** (structured / formal) or **open** (unstructured / informal). A closed list of specific questions enables the data to be processed easily and standardises the research. However, weaknesses are that respondents are 'pigeon-holed' into answering particular questions (possibly inappropriate ones) and cannot speak for themselves. (**Semi-structured questionnaires** combine a mixture of both closed and open questions.)

- **Self-administered (or self-completion) questionnaires** are completed by the respondents without guidance from an interviewer. They can be sent by post or left with respondents and collected at a later date. The problem of **interviewer bias** is avoided (i.e. results being influenced by the personality and social style of the interviewer), cost is low, and a large geographical area can be covered. Weaknesses are that response rate is usually low (below 40%), and the questions / instructions may be misunderstood.

- **Interviews** can be conducted on a face-to-face basis or by telephone. This is a flexible way of obtaining information, and has a higher response rate than postal questionnaires. Respondents can be coaxed, and the meaning of questions clarified. However, weaknesses are that it is expensive and time consuming. Interviewer bias can limit both **reliability** (different interviewers may obtain different results) and **validity** (the overall truth of the research).

- **Case studies** are detailed studies of particular individuals, groups or institutions – for example the investigation of race relations in the St. Paul's district of Bristol by Ken Pryce in *Endless Pressure* (1979). Case studies have been used to test out general theories and can give greater insight than larger-scale studies. However, weaknesses are that generalisations cannot be drawn since the particular case studied may be untypical.

- **Longitudinal (or panel)** research involves studying a particular group of individuals over an extended period. While most sociological research is a 'snapshot' taken at a particular moment, longitudinal research shows how social processes change over time. A representative group of respondents is interviewed at regular intervals. However, its weaknesses are panel mortality (some respondents may disappear and / or lose interest), expense, and the possibility that respondents may become untypical as a result of being studied.

- Note: **panel conditioning or the Hawthorne Effect**. This term is derived from the research by Elton Mayo at the Hawthorne Works of the Western Electric Company in Chicago in the 1920s. The presence of researchers in the factory changed workers' behaviour.

- **Experiments** are usually carried out in laboratory conditions where behaviour can be examined under controlled conditions and hypotheses tested clinically and objectively. An example is the *Obedience to Authority* experiment (1974) by Stanley Milgram. (This found that 65% of his forty volunteers were willing to inflict apparently dangerous electric shocks of up to 450 volts on people when instructed to do so by individuals in authority.) However, weaknesses are that only a limited number of conditions can be simulated in a laboratory, people may behave untypically in an artificial environment, and the method raises the question of whether it is ethical to carry out experiments on human beings.

- **Field experiments** are carried out in ordinary social contexts – for example, a study of social class conducted on Paddington railway station which compared responses to a request for directions when wearing a suit and bowler hat with responses to the same request when wearing labouring clothes.

- **Official statistics** published by various government departments are an example of secondary data. These provide large quantities of easily accessible information which

You need to be able to distinguish between **validity** and **reliability**.

The Hawthorne Effect is a major problem in sociological research.

may have been expensive to produce. (The cost of the 1991 census was around £135 million.) They may be the only source of data available on some subjects. However, weaknesses are that statistics may not have been collected in a reliable and consistent way, may reflect bias and prejudice, and can be subjected to political manipulation and 'packaging.'

Official statistics must be handled with care!

5 Factors influencing choice of research method

- **Theoretical perspective:** if a researcher has a positivist approach the aim will be to measure behaviour as objectively as possible using quantitative methods (such as structured social surveys). If a researcher has an anti-positivist approach the aim will be to study the subjective meanings which underpin behaviour and to probe feelings and intentions – using qualitative methods (such as ethnographic research).

- **What is being studied:** the subject matter of the research may determine which methods are used. For example, covert participant observation may be the only way of studying a deviant group.

- **Who is carrying out the study:** a researcher investigating members of an élite group who has personal connections with the élite will be able to use different methods from a researcher who lacks such connections.

- **Practical constraints:** if limited time is available for the research some methods (e.g. longitudinal studies) will have to be excluded. If limited money is available some methods (e.g. large-scale social surveys) will be unsuitable. Those who fund and publish research investigations may be more sympathetic to some types and styles of research than others.

- **Chance factors:** the quality of research investigations can be enhanced by 'opportunist' methods. (e.g. making full use of chance contacts and unexpected openings).

- **Action research:** methods are chosen which maximise the researcher's effectiveness as a 'change agent.' i.e. as someone who engages in research in order to change the lives of those s/he is studying rather than simply observing them.

6 Triangulation

Methodological pluralists use more than one method.

- This consists of using more than one method of research and is sometimes called **methodological pluralism**. If a number of different research approaches are used the weaknesses of one method can be countered by the strengths of another and a more complete picture of social reality can be built up.

- The use of triangulation signals a partial truce in the 'theory wars', a recognition that a variety of approaches – both quantitative and qualitative – can be used to advance sociological understanding.

- Critics of triangulation point out that in some research investigations the results obtained from one method have contradicted the results obtained from another method. Realism alerts us to the complexities involved in probing social reality. Triangulation does not provide an 'automatic fix' to the problems of research.

Controversy surrounds the use of covert methods.

- An example of a study which used triangulation is Eileen Barker's *The Making of a Moonie* (1984). This investigated the Unification Church founded in Korea by the Reverend Sun Myung Moon in 1954. Barker used three main methods: 1. in-depth interviews with thirty members of the Church; 2. living as a participant member in various Unification centres; 3. designing a questionnaire which was completed by 380 Moonies in Britain. The study found that a high proportion of Moonies had attended church during early childhood and that the majority of members were male, middle class, and unmarried. Barker did not reveal to the Moonies that she was a sociologist and gave the impression of being a 'true believer'. The British Sociological Association declared that such covert techniques of investigation are unethical.

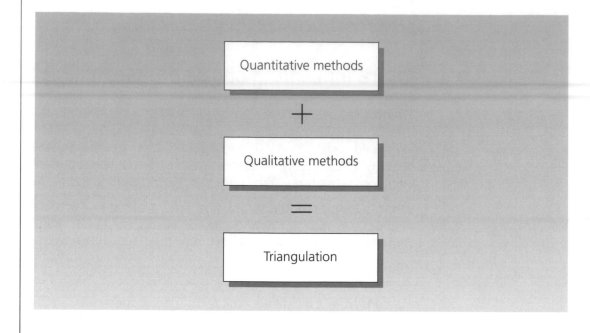

7 Overview of participant observation

Its strengths are that it:

- is naturalistic – individuals are studied in their ordinary environment, thus avoiding the artificiality of interview situations

- has a high level of validity – what respondents admit to doing in questionnaires may not correspond to their behaviour in real life

- allows spontaneous activity to be observed which would be missed if individuals were interviewed as isolated individuals

- provides a vivid picture of motives and values, and may be the only practical way of studying groups which are seen as deviant by the wider society.

Its weaknesses are that:

- it is very time consuming

- much depends on the reliability of the observer's analysis

- a study cannot be replicated (repeated)

- intense personal involvement may lead to a loss of objectivity

- the group studied may be unrepresentative and few (if any) generalisations can be drawn

- the participant observer might change the behaviour of those s/he is studying (Hawthorne Effect)

- in order to gain credibility with the group the researcher might feel under pressure to engage in illegal or dangerous activity

- if the study is covert it would breach the British Sociological Association's ethical guidelines.

Different participant observers will probably reach different conclusions.

8 | Overview of social surveys

The strengths are that:

- they deliver objective, accurately measured, 'scientific' data which can be easily put into statistical form

- they provide a high degree of reliability – if the survey is replicated the same results should be obtained

- by studying large numbers of respondents and using effective sampling techniques generalisations can be drawn

- the quality of data is not dependent on the personal impressions, skills, and objectivity of a single researcher

- research can be completed over a short time-span and at a low cost.

Social surveys are reliable but may lack validity.

Their weaknesses are that:

- the most important questions may not be asked

- the concepts and forms of language used in the survey may be misinterpreted, or the respondents may lie

- the high level of reliability of surveys (i.e. replication producing the same results) can be accompanied by low validity (i.e. a failure to convey a true picture of what is being studied)

- quantitative methods such as social surveys have been rejected by many feminists because 'they treat people as objects, as natural scientists treat chemicals or rocks, rather than as human subjects' – P. Abbott and C. Wallace *An Introduction To Sociology: Feminist Perspectives*, (1997).

9 | Checklist of key terms and concepts

Hypothetico deductive method   Hypothesis Theory   Verification and Falsification
Public knowledge   Natural science   *Verstehen*   Positivism   Paradigm   Realism
Value-relevance   Value-neutrality   Quantitative and Qualitative   Primary and secondary
sources   Representative sample   Ethnography   Covert and Overt   Interviewer bias
Reliability   Validity   Hawthorne Effect   Triangulation.

10 | Further reading

Harvey, L. and Macdonald, M. (1993) *Doing Sociology. A Practical Introduction*, London, Macmillan.

McNeil, P. (1990) *Research Methods*, 2nd edition, London, Tavistock.

Morison, M. (1986) *Methods in Sociology*, London, Longman.

Slattery, M. (1986) *Official Statistics*, London, Tavistock.

Chapter four

Social divisions and class stratification

1 | Key terms

- **Social inequality:** valued resources, rewards, and life-chances are unequally distributed on the basis of class / gender / ethnicity / age. There is unequal access to the '3 Ps' of power, prestige, and economic privilege.

- **Social stratification:** enduring hierarchical divisions of inequality.

- **Power:** the capacity to achieve goals and / or control the actions of others, even if they resist.

- **Prestige:** status or social standing.

- **Economic privilege:** access to and control of wealth and income.

- **Life chances:** the material advantages and cultural opportunities that are typically available / non-available for members of a particular group or class.

Remember the 3 P's.

2 | Systems of social stratification

- **Slavery:** In ancient civilisations such as Egypt and Rome, slaves were treated as property and revolts by slaves were cruelly punished. From the 16th to 19th centuries between 10 and 20 million Africans were transported across the Atlantic to plantations in the Caribbean and southern USA.

- **Caste:** The Indian caste system is the most enduring stratification system. Only through reincarnation can an individual hope to change his / her caste position. The main castes are Brahmins (priests), kshatriyas (warriors), vaishyas (traders), and shudras (servants and labourers). The untouchables are at the bottom of the caste hierarchy.

- **Estates:** In the feudal system of medieval Europe society was divided into three estates – the aristocracy, the clergy (priests), and commoners (peasants) – each with different legal rights. In traditional (pre-1868) Japan there were six main social orders – the Imperial family, great lords, warriors, peasants, artisans, and merchants. Important divisions existed within each order.

- **Class:** Use of the word 'class' dates from the Industrial Revolution. However, Aristotle (384–322 BC) believed that in all states there are 'three parts, or classes, of the citizen body – the very rich, the very poor; and the middle class…'.

Systems of stratification use different ideologies to legitimise inequality.

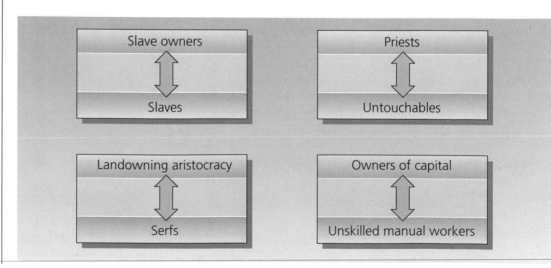

3 | Theories of Class

3.1 Marx's Theory of Class

- Marx never completed his theory of class. Chapter 23 of Volume 3 of *Capital* headed 'Classes' is unfinished. Clearly he sees the class structure of capitalist society as essentially **dichotomous** – there are two fundamental classes.

- These two classes are the **bourgeoisie** and the **proletariat**.

- Ownership and control of the means of production is the primary source of power and wealth.

3.2 Weber

Weber is the 'Marx of the Bourgeoisie'.

Weber was born forty-six years after Marx, and made the following criticisms of Marx's theory:

- The class structure of capitalist society has become more complex rather than polarising into two classes as Marx predicted.

- Position in the economic market place – not relationship to the means of production – is the defining feature of class (e.g. neither a factory manager nor a factory labourer own the means of production, but this does not mean they belong to the same class).

- Class refers to the economic order, status refers to the social order. Status groups are 'communities' which generate a sense of belonging and have distinctive patterns of consumption and life-style.

3.3 Marx versus Weber

Both Marx and Weber agreed that the concept of class was essentially economic. However,

Marx would criticise Weber for:

Weber believed that the dictatorship of the official – not the worker was on the march.

- giving insufficient recognition to the power which flows from ownership of the means of production

- over-playing the significance of status differences and under-playing the extent to which these are shaped by economic factors

- pessimistically accepting the inevitability of capitalism rather than trying to work towards its transformation.

Weber would criticise Marx for:

- failing to see that the middle class was expanding, not shrinking, and that class divisions were becoming less polarised

- over-estimating the likelihood of the working class becoming class conscious and politically organised – rather than remaining unaware of its potential for collective action

- believing that history was poised to take a 'great leap forward' in human emancipation. (Weber had an anti-utopian and pessimistic view of the future.)

3.4 Neo-Marxist approaches

- **Harry Braverman** – *Labour and Monopoly Capital. The Degradation of Work in the 20th Century* (1974). Proletarianisation' is taking place and workers are being deskilled and subjected to increasing managerial control. 'The apparent trend to a large non-proletarian "middle class" has resolved itself into the creation of a large proletariat in a new form.'

- **Eric O. Wright** – *Classes, Crisis and the State* (1978). Small employers, professionals, managers and supervisors occupy **contradictory class locations**. They do not own significant amounts of capital – so they have one foot in the proletariat. But they exercise authority and have economic privileges – so they have one foot in the bourgeoisie. They are at one and the same time both exploiters and exploited. Wright is a 'Weberian Marxist' accepting Weber's emphasis on the complexity of class stratification but subscribing to core Marxist concepts of class domination and exploitation.

Increasing numbers of individuals occupy contradictory class locations.

3.5 Neo-Weberian approaches

- **Anthony Giddens** – *The Class Structure of the Advanced Societies* (1973). Membership of the upper class depends on ownership of capital; membership of the middle class depends on possession of educational credentials; membership of the working class depends on possession of labour power.

- **Frank Parkin** – *Marxism and Class Theory: A bourgeois critique* (1979). Weber's emphasis on market opportunities and life chances has now been absorbed into Marxist theory. This constitutes 'a handsome, if unacknowledged tribute to the virtues of bourgeois sociology'.

4 | Classifications of class

Official definitions of class are un-sociological.

- **The Registrar-General's Classification.** In the ten-yearly census of population between 1911 and 1991 the economically active population was divided into Class 1 (professional); Class 2 (intermediate); Class 3 which is subdivided into two: skilled non-manual and skilled manual; Class 4 (semi-skilled manual); Class 5 (unskilled manual). Critics say that the classification is based on status, not class; it reflects a 'sexist' bias being based on the occupation of the 'male head of the household'; it ignores the 40% of the population who do not have paid employment; it places the 'super rich' in the same class as modestly paid professionals.

- **The Standard Occupational Classification.** This new official classification will replace the Registrar-General's Classification. Occupations will be divided into nine groups according to qualifications and skill levels. However, individuals who are 'not part of the formal economy' will continue to be ignored by the revised classification, e.g. those who are 'in education, retired, unemployed, housewives, sick and disabled, or institutionalised', Andy Barnard and Terry Burgess, *Sociology Explained* (1996).

- **The Goldthorpe Classification** – John Goldthorpe *Social Mobility and Class Structure in Modern Britain* (1987). Based on both market situation (e.g. income) and work situation (e.g. degree of authority / autonomy in the workplace). The **Service Class** is made up of Class I (higher-grade professionals, managers, etc.) and Class II (lower-grade professionals, etc.); the **Intermediate Class** is made up of Class III (routine non-manual, etc.), Class IV (small proprietors, etc.), and Class V (lower-grade technicians, supervisors of manual workers, etc.); the **Working Class** is made up of Class VI (skilled manual workers) and Class VII (semi and unskilled manual workers, etc.)

Objective definitions of class may not coincide with subjective definitions of class.

- **Note: Subjective and Objective Approaches to Class** Objective approaches classify individuals into particular classes on the basis of such factors as occupation, wealth, income, or education. Subjective approaches ask people to classify themselves by stating which class they feel they belong to. Marxists use the term **false consciousness** to describe the thinking of individuals who place themselves in a class which does not correspond to their 'objective' class position (e.g. a factory labourer who thinks he is middle class). Interactionists such as W.I. Thomas point out that subjective perceptions can alter objective reality: 'If men define situations as real, they are real in their consequences'.

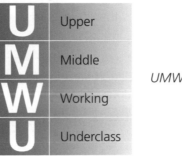

UMWU – class in Britain

5 | The class structure in Britain

5.1 The 'underclass'

Is the underclass a sociological or an ideological concept?

- The New Right theorist Charles Murray describes the underclass as 'The New Rabble': and predicts a growing divide between 'a working class, probably skilled, consisting predominantly of two-parent families' and a 'less skilled, predominantly unmarried working class...', *Underclass: The Crisis Deepens*, (1994).

- In the view of Anthony Giddens 'a major line of demarcation within the working class is between the ethnic majority and underprivileged minorities – who compose an underclass. Members of the underclass have markedly worse work conditions and living standards than the majority of the population. Many are among the long-term unemployed, or drift in and out of jobs. In Britain, blacks and Asians are disproportionately represented in the underclass' – *Sociology*, (1997).

- Stephen Edgell argues that the underclass is *not* a distinct class but forms *part* of the working class. It has a shifting rather than a static population and is essentially 'the underemployed and unemployed fraction of the working class...', *Class* (1993).

- In the view of Andy Pilkington the underclass thesis has 'heavily overstated the concentration of ethnic minorities in non-skilled work' and there is 'too much economic diversity to enable us to speak, unproblematically, of a black underclass', *Sociology Review* February 1992.

- It is widely accepted that social divisions have increased over recent decades, the demand for unskilled workers has declined, and the numbers of one-parent families and long-term unemployed have grown. However, the New Right thesis – that as a result of these changes a 'pathological' underclass has come into existence – has evoked fierce controversy. Some sociologists believe the term 'underclass' gives a negative label to an already marginalised section of society.

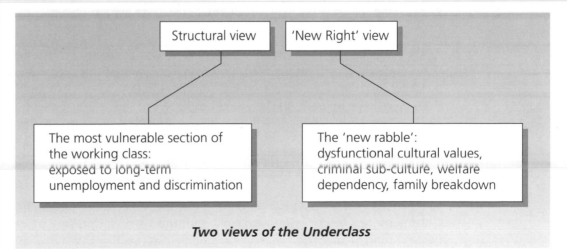

Two views of the Underclass

5.2 The working class

- In 1900 over three-quarters of the economically active population were manual workers; by 1950 less than two-thirds were and by 1980 only half.

- Neo-Marxists define lower-grade white-collar employees as 'working class' e.g. Ralph Miliband in *Divided Societies* (1989) estimates that between two-thirds and three-quarters of the population are working class. Non-Marxists place white-collar employees in the Middle Class, but they recognise that 'in some respects, especially of work situation and privatised lifestyles, manual workers are indistinguishable from routine non-manual workers...' – N. Abercrombie and A. Warde (1994).

Only a minority of the labour force are defined as manual workers.

5.3 The affluent working class

- A classic study is *The Affluent Worker in the Class Structure* (1969) by J.H. Goldthorpe and D. Lockwood which looked at the *embourgeoisement thesis* that the most prosperous section of the working class was becoming middle class.

- The study was based in Luton – a prosperous area with a high proportion of geographically mobile workers, many of whom had moved there because of the high wages. Workers at three companies were interviewed: assembly line workers at Vauxhall Motors, machine operators at the Skefko Ball Bearing Company, and process workers at Laporte Chemicals.

- The study examined three things: economic (e.g. were the workers' income, security, and promotion prospects on a par with the middle class?); relational (e.g. did they mix with middle-class people?); attitudinal and normative (e.g. were they acquiring middle-class norms and values?).

The embourgeoisement thesis was disproved.

- The affluent workers were found to have an 'instrumental orientation' to work. Job satisfaction was low and work merely a means to enable the purchase of consumer goods.

- The social life of the workers was privatised (home and family centred). There was a sharp dichotomy (split) between work and non-work. 'Mates are not friends.' There was no evidence of a shift towards support for the Conservative Party. 80% voted for the Labour Party.

- The embourgeoisement thesis was rejected. When security, fringe benefits, and life-time earnings were considered, the professional middle class was significantly better off in economic terms. There was no sign that leisure time was spent socialising with middle-class individuals. There was a strong element of 'status dissent' from middle-class values.

The Luton workers were instrumental collectivists.

- The affluent workers were not 'embourgeoisified' but *were* distinct from the traditional workers found in coal mining and dock communities. They had a more instrumental approach to work and led a more privatised and less community-based life. A divide was opening up between the *new* (skilled / affluent) working class and the *old* (less well-off / traditional in outlook) working class.

- In the 1980s Fiona Devine interviewed 62 Luton residents who were either Vauxhall workers or their wives. Lifestyles were less privatised, consumer aspirations more modest, and attitudes to work less instrumental than recorded in the original research study. Devine claims that Goldthorpe and Lockwood 'exaggerated the extent of change in working-class lifestyles between the first and second halves of the twentieth century', 'Affluent Workers Revisited', *Sociology Review*, February 1994.

5.4 The middle class

- The middle class can be divided into two unequal sections: the upper-middle class and routine white-collar workers – with the latter having very much poorer work and market situations than upper-middle class workers.

- Rather than speaking of *the* middle class we should be speaking of the middle *classes* because 'the white-collar range extends from the clerk in the town hall to the managing director, whereas blue-collar earnings are relatively compressed' – Abercrombie and Warde (1994).

- Sociological research has neglected the study of 'prosperous suburbia' – even though the middle classes make up over half of the population.

- A classic study of middle-class occupations was *The Blackcoated Worker* (1958) by David Lockwood. A Marxist definition puts both the bank clerk and the labourer in the working class since neither owns the means of production. However, Lockwood found that the market (income), job (degree of autonomy) and status (prestige) positions of the clerk were markedly superior to that of the labourer.

- The key sectors of the middle classes are: the **upper-middle class** of top managers, large business owners and professionals; the **old middle class** of small business owners; the **new middle class** of semi-professionals (such as teachers and social workers) and the **lower-middle class** of routine white-collar workers.

5.5 The upper class

- The upper class – the top 1 per cent of wealth-holders – comprises three main sectors: the entrepreneurial rich who own stocks and shares, the land-owning rich, and the 'jet-set' rich involved in entertainment, sport and the media. Status divisions exist between 'new' and 'old' money, A. Giddens, *Sociology* (1997).

- John Scott – *Who Rules Britain?* (1991) estimates that the core of the upper class consists of some 43,500 people (0.1% of the population) who together own 7% of the wealth and are connected by networks of marriage, kinship, and friendship.

- The process of 'assortive mating' – the tendency for people to marry individuals from similar social backgrounds (endogamy rather than exogamy) – reinforces the cohesion of the upper class and increases economic inequality.

- C. Harbury and D. Hitchens in *Inheritance and Wealth Inequality in Britain* (1979) found that 'over 60% of top wealth leavers were preceded by rich fathers.'

- Ralph Miliband believes the 'dominant class' consists of the power élite (those who take major political decisions and wield state power), owners of large and medium-sized firms, higher professionals, and 'opinion leaders'. All members of the dominant class are 'at the upper levels of the income and ownership scale'.

6 The debate on the Managerial Revolution

- In *The Managerial Revolution* (1941) James Burnham argued that power in industrial societies was passing into the hands of professional managers; ownership was being divorced from control; key decisions in companies were no longer being taken by the owners. (The 'de-composition of capital' thesis.)

- The power of the capitalist class is fragmenting, the upper class is merging with the middle class, and managerial decisions are guided by a sense of social responsibility rather than the pursuit of profit.

- Critics of this view argue: 1. Some large companies are still owned and controlled by their founding families; 2. The goal of both owners and managers is long-term maximisation of profits, not the creation of a 'caring capitalism'; 3. Many top managers hold substantial shareholdings in their companies – they are part-owners as well as managers; 4. Owners and managers tend to share the same values and come from similar social backgrounds; 5. Networks of interlocking directorships reinforce the cohesion of the upper class (e.g. the director of a bank may also sit on the boards of other companies and corporations).

7 | Social mobility

Trace the mobility pattern of your own family.

- **Social mobility:** the movement of individuals and groups between different positions in the social hierarchy.

- **Vertical mobility:** movement up or down the social hierarchy. The upwardly mobile gain wealth and status, the downwardly mobile lose wealth and status.

- **Inter-generational social mobility:** a change in status from one generation to the next.

- **Intra-generational social mobility:** a change of status within an individual's own lifetime.

- **Sponsored mobility:** recruits into the élite are selected by the élite. (What counts is *who you know.*)

- **Contest mobility:** recruits into the élite are selected in an open contest on the basis of their ability and achievement rather than ascribed (inherited) status. (What counts is *what you know.*)

- **Meritocracy:** a system in which status is achieved on the basis of merit ('intelligence plus effort') rather than ascribed on the basis of inherited position. The term was coined by Michael Young in *The Rise of the Meritocracy* (1958).

- **Lateral (or geographical) mobility:** movement between different neighbourhoods /areas / cities, etc.

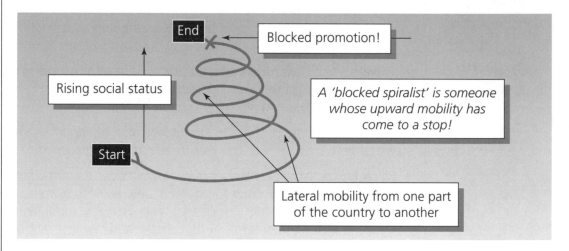

8 | Key studies

8.1 Social Mobility in Britain (1954) by David Glass

The Britain studied by Glass was a relatively closed society.

- This pioneering research was based on a random sample of 10,000 adult males living in England, Scotland, and Wales in 1949. Occupations of respondents were compared with those of their fathers. Most mobility was short range rather than long range, and was concentrated at the middle of the class structure.

8.2 Social Mobility in Industrial Societies (1959) by S.M. Lipset and R. Bendix

- A comparative study of mobility patterns in nine countries. Vertical male mobility rates were found to be very similar. In the USA 30% of the sons of manual workers moved into non-manual occupations compared with 31% in West Germany, 29% in Sweden and Britain and 27% in France and Japan.

- Social mobility acted as a **safety valve** which reduced the likelihood of radical political action.

- **Status inconsistency** generated resentment in some individuals. This was because they had high status on one dimension (e.g. they were wealthy) but had low status on another dimension (e.g. they came from a low-status ethnic background).

- The study quoted the Austrian sociologist Joseph Schumpeter: 'each social class resembles a hotel or omnibus, always full, but always of different people.'

8.3 The Oxford Mobility Study (OMS) – Social Mobility and Class Structure in England and Wales (1988) by J. Goldthorpe, C. Llewellyn, and C. Payne

The Britain studied by the OMS had become a more open society.

- The major research study of social mobility in Britain. Based on a survey conducted in 1972 of 10,000 men aged between 20 and 24. Mobility levels (including long-range mobility) were significantly higher than those which existed in 1949.

- The decline in blue-collar jobs and the expansion in white-collar jobs (especially managerial and professional positions) had created 'more room at the top,' with three-quarters of the men in the top 'service class' experiencing upward mobility. However, critics point out that the service class comprises 12% of men in work which is too broad to tell us much about the chances of reaching the very top.

- There was no evidence to support the existence of a **buffer-zone** (a fault line between blue-collar and white-collar occupations which acts as a brake on social mobility).

- The **closure thesis** was rejected (this sees the top class as largely self-recruiting). The highest degree of social closure and homogeneity (similarity of social background) was found at the bottom of the class structure. 'If one was to take a manual worker at random from the present-day population, the chances would be greater than 3 in 4 that he would be a second-generation blue collar.'

- Despite increased social mobility, inequalities in opportunity remain deeply entrenched. The **1:2:4 Rule of Relative Hope** continues to apply: whatever chance a working-class boy has of making it into the top service class, a boy from the middle intermediate class has twice the chance, and a boy from the service class has four times the chance.

8.4 Social Mobility (1981) by Anthony Heath

Research on social mobility has been research on male social mobility.

- Notes that every major research survey of mobility has been based on a 'men only' sample. Past researchers have argued that the majority of husbands and wives share the same class position, and the man was usually the main breadwinner. But today many one-parent families are headed by women, and in some households the woman is the only wage-earner. It will no longer be credible for future mobility studies to exclude women.

- Dramatic inequalities still exist between the élite and the non-élite. An individual from a working-class home has about 1 chance in 1,500 of getting into *Who's Who* (which lists members of the élite) while an individual from an élite home has a 1 in 5 chance.

8.5 Social Class in Modern Britain (1988) by Gordon Marshall, *et al*.

- 'Perhaps as many as one-third of those presently in service-class positions have arrived there from working-class origins... Upward mobility on this scale is clearly at odds with Marxist theories about the rigidity of class structures in advanced capitalism. Nor can these theories be salvaged by recourse to arguments about the proletarianisation of the middle layers of the structure. There is nothing in our data to suggest that routine non-manual jobs, or those who perform them, are somehow degraded or deskilled.'

- However there are 'serious flaws' in the liberal view that Britain now has an open and fluid class structure. An individual born into the top service-class is between seven and thirteen times more likely to get a service-class job than an individual born into the working class.

9 | The Functionalist view of inequality

- K. Davis and W.E. Moore (1945) view social inequality as 'the device by which society ensures that the most important positions are filled by the most qualified persons.' This is because:

- certain occupations are functionally more important than others

- only a limited number of people are sufficiently talented to be able to perform these occupations competently

- in order to persuade talented people to undergo the training needed for important occupations they must be offered an incentive. i.e. higher than average salaries,

- thus in all societies social inequality is inevitable and functional. If everyone was paid the same there would be no incentive for talented individuals to study and train for qualifications. Money continues to be the key motivator for the vast majority of people.

10 | The Marxist view of inequality

- The analysis of Davis and Moore is an ideologically loaded attempt at legitimising inequality. It attempts to convince the economically disadvantaged that they deserve to be so since they (supposedly) lack the special talents possessed by those in well-paid jobs.

- Many individuals achieve top occupations as a result of privileged educational opportunities and favourable social backgrounds rather than because of their special talents.

- Long periods of training and study required to gain qualifications are not a real sacrifice. Being a student may sometimes be a self-actualising and fulfilling experience.

- Individuals can be motivated by other than monetary considerations, e.g. a sense of social duty, or the prospect of high job satisfaction, or status, can be incentives for studying and training.

- Davis and Moore ignore the fact that economic inequalities can produce 'negative dysfunctions' such as high crime rates and poverty.

- It is impossible to objectively measure the contribution different jobs make to society (e.g. in 1997 a fund manager at Morgan Grenfell was paid £1.15 million a year. Can it be 'proved' that the functional contribution of this job is 60 times greater than that of a further education lecturer?)

Marxists believe in equality.

11 | The debate on class divisions

- '...middle-class people in those days took what was almost a Hindu view of society, which they held to consist of sharply defined castes, so that everyone at his birth found himself called to that station in life which his parents already occupied, and from which nothing, save the accident of an exceptional career or a 'good' marriage could extract you and translate you to a superior caste', *Remembrance of Things Past*, Marcel Proust (1913–27).

- 'Forget the past. No more bosses and workers. We are on the same side.' (Tony Blair, speech to the Labour Party Conference, October 1996.)

11.1 View 1 – Britain is becoming a *less* class-divided society

- 'Britain is much more meritocratic than is generally believed' writes Peter Saunders, *Unequal But Fair? A Study of Class Barriers in Britain* (1996). 'In modern Britain, if you are bright and committed, you are likely to succeed in the occupational system irrespective of where you start out from, and although things are not perfect and the playing field is not completely level, this means that our society is nevertheless remarkably open...'

- Data from the Oxford Mobility Study, Marshall's research at Essex University, and Payne's research in Scotland, all confirm that there is substantial upward and downward mobility. Working-class children are three to four times less likely to achieve middle-class jobs than middle-class children, but in Saunder's view this could be explained by their 'lower average intelligence.'

- Consumer living standards for the majority of the population have increased dramatically, and class divisions are being replaced by lifestyle choices. We now live in a media-saturated, highly individualistic, and possibly 'post-modern' culture. Individuals can re-shape their identities through shopping, fashion, travel, and use of the media. Age, gender, and ethnicity now have a greater influence than collective class identities.

- Saunders believes the capitalist class in Britain 'has all but disappeared as a distinct stratum'. Both the salaried section of the middle class and the lower middle class have expanded, while the working class has contracted and become more affluent. While at the bottom of the class structure is a small and marginalised underclass. Saunders challenges the view that class inequality is self-evidently a 'bad thing'. Inequality 'is the price to be paid for future growth from which all can benefit' and social justice 'has just as much to do with how people come by what they have got as with how much or how little they end up with' – *Social Class and Stratification* (1990).

Intelligence + effort = upward mobility.

11.2 View 2: Britain *continues* to be a class-divided society

- A. B. Atkinson, *Unequal Shares* (1972), found that 'In 1969, 19 people died leaving estates of over £1 million, an amount it would have taken the average manual worker a thousand years to earn.' In his *Parade Of The Dwarfs And The Giants* Jan Pen made height proportionate to income, with the average income being given the average height. As this imaginary parade passes by, old age pensioners stand three feet high, skilled manual workers four feet high, top civil servants thirty-nine feet high, and the super rich over a mile high.

- Research by the Joseph Rowntree Foundation (1995) found that the gap between rich and poor was greater than at any time since 1945. Between 1979 and 1992 (after deducting for housing costs) the income of the bottom tenth of the population actually fell by 17%. An updated study published in 1998 found that the gap between rich and poor had marginally narrowed since 1992. But even if this trend continues 'it will take more than a decade to get back to where we were in the 1970s.'

- In 1979 there were some 1.2 million households in which no adults were in paid employment. The Labour Force Survey found that by the end of 1995 this had increased to 3.3 million. One in five households now have no income earner.

1990s Britain is a more unequal society than 1970s Britain – which was a highly unequal society.

- Class divisions have actually *deepened* in Britain in recent decades. The gap between the bottom tenth and the rest of the population has widened. Anthony Giddens points out that the social isolation which separates underprivileged groups from the rest of the social order within nations mirrors the division of the rich from the poor on a global scale.

12 | Checklist of key terms and concepts

- Social Inequality   Social differentiation   Social stratification   Life chances   Dichotomous   Class and status   Class in itself   Class for itself   Proletarianisation   Contradictory class locations   Subjective and Objective approaches   Embourgeoisement   Instrumental   New and Old Working Class   Privatised   Meritocracy   Inter-generational and Intra-generational   Vertical and Lateral mobility   Sponsored mobility   Contest mobility   Status inconsistency   Buffer-zone   Closure Thesis   1:2:4 Rule of Relative Hope

13 | Further reading

Abercrombie, N. and Warde, A. (1994) *Contemporary British Society. A New Introduction to Sociology*, Cambridge, Polity.

Abercrombie, N. and Warde, A. (eds) (1994) *Stratification and Social Inequality: Studies in British Society*, Lancaster, Framework Press.

Edgell, S. (1993) *Class*, London, Routledge.

Scase, R. (1992) *Class*, Milton Keynes, Open University Press.

Culture, identity and youth

1 | Culture and identity

1.1 Key terms

- *Culture:* the way of life of a society. 'That complex whole which includes knowledge, belief, art, morals, law, custom, and any other capabilities and habits acquired by man as a member of society – Edward Tylor – *Primitive Culture* (1891). Culture includes not only 'high culture' but all aspects of a society's way of life, its norms (social rules) and values (principles and ideals).

- *Sub-culture:* a culture within a culture, the way of life of a particular group.

- *Identity:* a continuous sense of self and personhood. The Latin root of identity is *identitas* from *idem* – 'the same'.

- *Reflexivity:* the capacity of individuals to reflect upon the consequences of their own actions and to modify their identities.

1.1 Formation of identity

- Identity is formed in the process of socialisation. Society 'builds itself into our personalities and teaches us specific ways of acting, thinking, and feeling' – S. Cotgrove – *The Science of Society* (1967).

- Feral children (reared in the wild by wolves or other animals) lack a recognisably 'human' personality. They illustrate the formative impact of early socialisation.

- In 1939 Norman Elias introduced the concept of the *civilising process*. Expectations of behaviour in everyday life have changed significantly over the last few centuries, (e.g. in the Middle Ages belching and excreting in public were not regarded as 'bad manners').

- G. H. Mead (1863–1931) and other **symbolic interactionists** show how identity is shaped in a dynamic process of interaction. Richard Jenkins analyses identity in terms of a continuum, with an individual's **self-image** at one end and **public image** at the other.

- **Functionalists** such as **Talcott Parsons** (1902–1979) see the family as playing a crucial role in the formation of identity. The family is likened to an 'assembly line' which produces human personalities with specific cultural predispositions.

Culture is more than just high culture.

Reflexivity is now a key concept in Sociology.

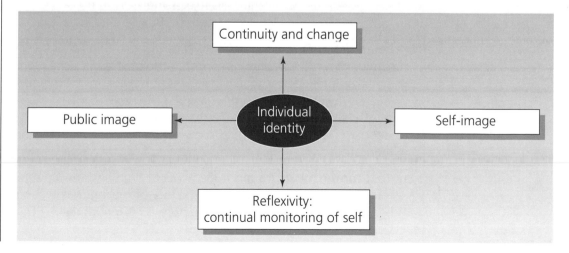

- **Neo-Marxists** such as **Antonio Gramsci** (1891–1937) believe that the hegemony (cultural leadership) of the dominant class exerts a powerful influence on 'common sense' ideas of identity. The Centre for Contemporary Cultural Studies established at Birmingham University in the mid-1960s attempted to apply Gramsci's ideas to the study of popular culture.

- **Feminists** see patriarchal ideology (beliefs which support the dominance of men over women) as having a powerful influence on gender relations. Men have a vested interest in the existing patriarchal structure.

- **Post-modernists** claim that individuals are becoming decentred and no longer have fixed identities or 'grounded' selves. The growth of 'fundamentalist' social movements can be seen as an attempt at recapturing a 'cast-iron' and unproblematic sense of who individuals are.

- Stuart Hall distinguishes between three concepts of identity:

  1 **The enlightenment subject.** Based on the view of the human person as 'a fully centred, unified individual. . . . whose 'centre' consisted of an inner core which first emerged when the subject was born, and unfolded with it, while remaining essentially the same . . . throughout the individual's existence.'

  2 **The sociological subject.** The individual 'as autonomous and self-sufficient...(but) formed in relation to "significant others" ... Identity in this sociological conception bridges the gap between the "inside" and the "outside" – between the personal and the public worlds.'

  3. **The post-modern subject.** The self is fragmented. 'Identity becomes a "moveable feast": formed and transformed continuously in relation to the ways we are represented or addressed in the cultural systems which surround us', 'The Question of Cultural Identity' in *Modernity and Its Futures* (1992).

2 | Types of culture

- When **culture** was defined by Matthew Arnold as 'the best that has been thought and said in the world,' what Arnold had in mind was high or élite culture – the culture of a highly educated minority.

- **Folk culture** refers to the culture of the population of pre-industrial rural society. T.S. Eliot put forward a nostalgic view of the spiritually enriching character of folk culture, and he contrasts this with the impoverished character of modern mass culture. (Eliot also gave a 'neo-functionalist' justification for inequality: without the existence of leisured and privileged élites the precious legacy of high culture would have been lost.)

- **Mass culture** is commercially produced in standardised forms and is designed to appeal to the tastes of large numbers of people. Theorists associated with the Frankfurt School (such as Theodor Adorno) saw mass culture as aesthetically inferior to high culture. But Paul Willis rejects the view that mass culture is 'inferior to 'cultured' culture', *Moving Culture* (1990).

- **Relativist** approaches to culture ('it is not possible to judge one culture as objectively superior') can be distinguished from absolutist approaches to culture (some cultures are 'absolutely better than others') – Paul Taylor, *Investigating Culture and Identity* (1997). Taylor notes that most sociologists take an intermediate position: **soft relativism**: 'we need to be cautious about judging other cultures by our own standards while insisting that some claims to truth rest on more scientific evidence than others.'

- **Post-modern culture** mixes elements of high and low culture in new and innovative forms. A 'profound shift in the structure of feeling' has taken place and the distinction between high culture and mass culture is no longer valid – David Harvey – *The Condition of Postmodernity* (1996).

From grounded self to de-centred self.

Is 'cultured culture' superior to 'mass culture'?

- **Popular culture** 'can be seen as the cultural activity that emerges from "the people" . . . including . . . challenging their consensual role as recipients of an imposed culture.' It can represent a form of hegemonic struggle. In the view of some theorists 'what has been traditionally seen as "mass culture" is better described as "popular culture", where cultural activity that has traditionally been seen as being imposed from above becomes seen as working-class people gaining "cultural space" for themselves, and transforming ideas and artefacts for their own purposes' – Andy Barnard and Terry Burgess – *Sociology Explained* (1996).

3 | Cultural sources of identity

3.1 Class

- According to the historian De Ste. Croix, class position (based on control and ownership of property) has profoundly influenced individual identity, both in the ancient civilisations of Greece and Rome as well as in contemporary societies.

- French sociologist Pierre Bourdieu argues that personal tastes and cultural preferences are determined by the *habitus* or set of dispositions acquired from a particular social background. In a class society individuals have a 'sense of one's place' and this manifests itself in cultural likes and dislikes. Thus the kind of paintings which working-class people prefer differ from those preferred by lower middle-class people. Preferences in food, drinks, leisure activities, holidays, sport, music, and clothes also vary with class location. In Bourdieu's view, class shapes the most personal and individual aspects of identity and self: 'Every body is the bearer of signs – clothing, pronunciation, bearing, posture, manners...' – *Distinction. A Social Critique of the Judgement of Taste* (1984).

3.2 Gender

- Christine Griffin studied the experiences of young women in their first two years in employment after school and found that gender divisions exerted a powerful impact on individual identity. The sexual marketplace values women according to their perceived attractiveness to men, with youth at a particular premium. *Typical Girls? Young Women From School To The Job Market* (1985).

- Sue Cartledge in 1983 explored the emotional, practical and moral difficulties which are encountered in challenging patriarchal ideology and the concept of 'coupledom'.

- Roberta Hamilton believes that gender oppression has a more powerful impact on individual identity than class exploitation. Women in any social system bear 'the greater burden of perpetuating the species . . . Men have conquered the world because they had nature on their side' – *The Liberation of Women. A Study of Patriarchy and Capitalism* (1978).

- Naomi Woolf carried out a study of how girls 'become women' by interviewing female friends she had known at high school. Feminine identities are formed 'as a result of two pressures: the external – what their culture tells them it means to be an adult sexual female – and the internal – the development of sexual desire itself', *Promiscuities* (1997).

3.3 Ethnicity

- Identity is shaped by the shared beliefs and cultural practices of the ethnic group (or groups) an individual belongs to. Every individual has a distinctive ethnic identity. Paul Gilroy says of the black population in Britain 'There are significant differences of language, religion, ethnicity and culture evident within this population. In recent years it has come to be increasingly internally divided. It is economically stratified and politically split' – *Small Acts. Thoughts on the politics of black cultures* (1983). **Hybrid cultures** have emerged which combine practices and styles from numerous ethnic sources. Stuart Hall rejects the view that ethnic identity is fixed and enduring – individuals are continually 'negotiating different kinds of differences – of gender, of sexuality, of class' – Stuart Hall. *Critical Dialogues in Cultural Studies*, eds D. Morley and Kuan-Hsing Chen (1996).

- Robin Cohen argues that recognition of the existence of **multiple social identities** means that old essentialisms have to be discarded, e.g. 'the Marxist idea that all social identity could *essentially* be reduced to class identity.' Other forms of identity in addition to class include 'gender, age, disability, race, religion, ethnicity, nationality, civil status, even musical styles and dress codes...' The concept of 'British identity' includes 'Irish, Scots, Welsh and English people, those from the white, black or brown Commonwealth...' – *Frontiers of Identity. The British and the Others* (1994).

3.4 Nationalism

- Since the American and French Revolutions of the 18th century nationalism has powerfully influenced individual identity. Benedict Anderson defines a nation as an 'imagined community' – it is impossible for members of even a small nation to personally know most individuals of the same nationality, *Imagined Communities* (1983).

- Two different forms of nationalism can be distinguished: **civic** and **ethnic**. **Civic nationalism** maintains that 'the nation should be composed of all those – regardless of race, colour, creed, gender, language or ethnicity – who subscribe to the nation's political creed.' **Ethnic nationalism** claims that 'an individual's deepest attachments are inherited, not chosen' – nations are based on a 'people's pre-existing ethnic characteristics: their language, religion, customs and traditions,' Michael Ignatieff, *Blood and Belonging. Journeys into the New Nationalism* (1994).

- **Perennialists** believe that nations have always existed and are rooted in the distant past. **Modernists** believe that nations are an eighteenth-century invention. In the view of John Breuilly nations cannot simply be invented – there must be some ethnic base to work on. Eric Hobsbawm argues that nations and 'traditions' *can* simply be invented by organising public ceremonies, erecting monuments, setting up state education systems, etc.

- **Post-modernists** believe that global communications will weaken nationalism and generate new and more diverse forms of cultural identity. **Functionalists** believe that nationalist ideology provides individuals with a sense of identity and belonging and will continue to be reinforced by inter-state rivalries.

3.5 Values and ideology

- Functionalist analyst Talcott Parsons (who combined the approaches of Freud and Durkheim) argues that identity is shaped by the processes of socialisation and social control. Individuals internalise (absorb within their own psyches) the consensual values of the wider society.

- According to Marxist analysis the ideology disseminated by the ruling class has a powerful impact on individual identity. Critics of *The Dominant Ideology Thesis* (a book by N. Abercrombie *et al.* (1983)) argue that neo-Marxists have exaggerated the degree to which active ideological consent sustains the capitalist order. It is the pressures of everyday economic survival which lead most people to accept the status quo.

3.6 Individual reflexivity

- Anthony Giddens argues that we now live in a 'post-traditional order' and self-identity has become a 'reflexive project'. The forces of the modern world have broken down 'the protective framework of the small community and of tradition . . . The individual feels bereft and alone in a world in which she or he lacks the psychological supports and the sense of security provided by more traditional settings. Therapy offers someone to turn to, a secular version of the confessional', *Modernity and Self-Identity. Self and Society in the Late Modern Age* (1991).

- Chris Shilling believes the body has become increasingly significant for personal identity. 'If one feels unable to exert influence over an increasingly complex society, at least one can have some effect on the size, shape and appearance of one's body.' *The Body and Social Theory* (1993).

- Peter Saunders sees consumption as enabling people to exert some control over their lives. At work individuals are relatively powerless but in the shopping malls they can explore new facets of self. Consumer culture now exerts a far more pervasive influence on self-identity than was anticipated by the social commentators of forty years ago. Lauren Langman notes that among young people 'the various subcultures are clearly differentiated by the styles, fashions and tastes of particular stores, brands or regions of malldom...', *Shopping for Subjectivity*, in *Lifestyle Shopping. The Subject of Consumption*, edited by R. Shields (1992).

4 | Youth

- In pre-industrial societies there is no period of transition between childhood and adulthood. In medieval Europe a child was treated as 'mini-adult' and it was only from the 15th century on that members of the upper class began to dress their children in distinctive clothes. The concept of 'youth' was invented in industrial societies. In some cultures special rites of passage are held to mark the change from child to adult status.

4.1 Youth culture

- The term **youth culture** was coined by Talcott Parsons in 1942 to describe values and behaviour patterns which are distinct from those of adult society.

- **Youth sub-cultures** refer to sub-divisions within youth culture which are often related to social divisions of class and ethnicity. Although youth sub-cultures existed in the nineteenth century it was only in the 1950s that they acquired a high degree of public visibility.

- Only a minority of young people belong to a distinct youth sub-culture. 'The great majority of working-class youth never enters a tight or coherent subculture at all.' S. Hall and T. Jefferson (eds) – *Resistance Through Rituals. Youth subcultures in post-war Britain* (1976).

- Only a small minority of young people can be said to belong to a **contra-culture** – a sub-culture which rejects and is in basic conflict with the values of adult society.

4.2 Factors which led to the emergence of youth sub-cultures

- **Affluence:** teenagers' earnings in Britain doubled (in real terms) between 1939 and 1959. Much of this could be spent on entertainment, clothes etc. rather than on rent and mortgages.

- **Demographic change:** between 1958 and 1968 the number of teenagers increased by 20%.

- **Impact of the mass media:** television and advertising helped create a 'generational consciousness' (e.g. the 'hit parade' was invented in the USA in 1937).

- **Expansion of education:** dramatic increases in the numbers experiencing post-school education accelerated the growth in youth consciousness.

4.3 Theoretical approaches to youth sub-cultures

Simon Frith, *The Sociology of Youth* (1984) distinguishes between:

1 **Functionalist approaches:** in industrial societies young people have a marginal and 'in between' social status – they are neither adults or children. Support from peer groups helps individuals gain independence from their families. Youth culture is functional for the social system because it helps 'smooth out' the transition from childhood to adulthood. It is functional for young people because it generates a sense of belonging which helps meet their social and psychological needs.

2 **Meanings approaches:** studies carried out by the Centre for Contemporary Cultural Studies attempted to 'decipher' the social and political messages expressed in youth sub-cultural styles, (i.e. a **semiotic** approach – interpreting signs) e.g. the elegant dress style of the teddy boys in the 1950s was an attempt at closing the status gap between the lower and higher classes, and the skinhead style of the 1970s sought to re-create a sense of the traditional working-class community. Sub-cultural styles provide 'symbolic' and 'magical' solutions to social problems. Neo-Marxists see them as constituting 'rituals of resistance' against the established order. However 'resistance through ritualistic leisure pursuits does not really solve the problems of poor education and unemployment. The ability of youth cultures to resist dominant values is severely limited, and their artefacts are soon taken over by commercial interests and turned into mass consumer items' – A. Barnard and T. Burgess, *Sociology Examined* (1996).

4.4 Key studies

- Kenneth Leech's *Youthquake. The growth of a counter culture through two decades* (1973) gives a thumb-nail sketch of early youth sub-cultures in Britain. Leech argues that in their different ways, the Teds, Mods and Rockers, and Skinheads represented the conventional patterns of juvenile rebellion.

- Stanley Cohen in *Folk Devils and Moral Panics. The Creation of the Mods and Rockers* (1972) argues that youth culture 'is highly stratified along class, regional and educational lines and that 'the first pop heroes embodied the highly conservative values involved in the success stories of being discovered and making it...'

- Paul Willis, *Profane Culture* (1978) studied two very different youth sub-cultures: motorbike boys who 'were exploring and extending versions of "rough" working-class themes' and hippies who were 'exploring and broadening a middle-class tradition of the bohemian intelligentsia...'

- In *Hiding In The Light* (1988) Dick Hebdidge rejects the view that youth sub-cultures must be either the product of commercial manipulation or the authentic expression of non-conformity. Youth culture 'deals in the currency of signs and is, thus, always ambiguous... Sub-culture forms up the space between surveillance and the evasion of surveillance...It is a hiding in the light.'

- Paul Willis, 'Youth Unemployment, A New Social State', *New Society* (29.3.84): a 'new social condition' has been created in areas of high unemployment. Many young unemployed people exist in a state of 'suspended animation', a kind of marginal limbo-land. They lack the financial means of participating in a full social life and gaining independence from their parents.

- In 'Towards re-constructing a sociology of youth', *Social Science Teacher* (Summer

Youth culture provides an anchor for identity.

Semiotic approaches decipher the meaning of youth sub-cultural styles.

Youth culture is not uniform and homogeneous.

1986): Bob Coles states that youth culture research had focused on 'the glamorous fringe.' Female youth, black youth and 'ordinary youth' had been neglected.

- Angela McRobbie in 1991 drew attention to the 'complete absence of interest in girls' which characterised most youth culture research.

- Howard Parker et al. – Drugs Futures: changing patterns of drug use amongst English youth (1995) found that 51% of a sample of 700 young people in the north-west had tried drugs. 'Over the next few years, and certainly in urban areas, non drug-trying adolescents will be a minority group. In one sense, they will be the deviants...for many young people taking drugs has become the norm.'

- A report by the Joseph Rowntree Foundation in 1997 rejected the 'moral panic' view that a drug culture was sweeping Britain. 'The stereotype is that young drug users are sad losers, obsessive short-termists with no conception of their career, or that they lack any kind of moral sense. This applies only to a very small number of people.'

5 The 'old' and the 'new' sociology of youth

- The key focus of the 'old' sociology of youth is on the norms of the minority who participate in youth sub-cultures. The key focus of the 'new' sociology of youth is the social problems faced by ordinary young people (such as crime, cuts in benefits, unemployment, conditions on training schemes. etc.).

- The 'golden age' of youth culture between the 1950s and 1960s was a time of increasing affluence and leisure. From the 1970s the social situation of youth changed significantly. Between 1972 and 1977 the unemployment rate for those aged under 20 rose by 120% (three times as fast as the rise in the overall unemployment rate). Instead of 'dropping out' into a counter-culture increasing numbers of young people were 'dropping in' to the new Youth Training Schemes. By the late 1980s around 70% of 16-year-olds were joining YTS programmes. In 1986 unemployment rates for the under 24 age-group stood at 22%. In 1996 the unemployment rate for 18- and 19-year-olds was twice the national average.

- Changes in benefit regulations and a 'freeze' in council house building led to an increase in the numbers of homeless young people. In 1991 'youth riots' broke out in housing estates (e.g. in Cardiff and Tyneside) and social problems such as drug-taking, poverty, and crime intensified.

- There is a greater variety of subcultural styles in the 1990s than in the 1960s. Sarah Thornton argues that for 'a broad spectrum of British youth' going to dance clubs and participating in new 'taste cultures' is now an integral part of growing up. Steve Redhead has pointed to the oppositional elements in rave culture.

- Adults are more likely to be 'locked' into circumscribed routines than young people. Angela McRobbie points to the intensity of the processes of separation and detachment from parents and the simultaneous attachment to the symbols of freedom and adventure such as those provided in music and found in the spaces of the street and night-club', Postmodernism and Popular Culture (1994). Youth sub-cultures continue to have considerable influence on society.

6 Checklist of key terms and concepts

Norms Values Socialisation Reflexivity Feral children The civilising process
Elite culture Folk culture Mass culture Popular culture Decentring of self
Rites of passage Youth sub-culture Contra-culture Habitus Hybrid cultures
Multiple social identities Civic nationalism Ethnic nationalism

7 | Further Reading

Hutchinson, S. and Smith, A.D., (eds) (1994) *Nationalism*, Oxford, Oxford University Press.

McRobbie, A. (1994) *Postmodernism and Popular Culture*, London, Routledge.

Taylor, P. (1997) *Investigating Culture and Identity*, London, Collins Educational.

Trowler, P. (1984) *Topics in Sociology*, Slough, University Tutorial Press.

Chapter six

Mass media

1 | Definition

- 'The mass media communicate messages to large dispersed audiences through technological devices and reach large numbers of people at the same time', *The Complete A–Z Handbook* (1996) by T. Lawson and J. Garrod.

1.1 Historical development

- Printing was invented by Johann von Gutenberg in the 1450s, and introduced to Britain in 1476.

- Newspapers were published from the late 17th century onwards. The modern popular press dates from 1896 when the *Daily Mail* was launched. The 'golden age' of newspapers was 1930–47 when sales reached around 15.5 million a day. Today sales are around 14 million a day. 'Picture palaces' (cinemas) were opened from 1906 on, and cinema attendances reached a peak in the mid-1940s.

- The BBC began regular radio transmissions in 1936. In 1950 only 10% of homes had television sets; by 1963 only 10% were without. Television is the dominant medium of mass communication. Average weekly TV viewing time in the UK is 25.1 hours a week (26.5 hours in Central Scotland and 22.1 hours in the East of England). Women on average watch 26.5 hours, men on average 24 hours, *Sociology Update 1998*.

- 'Imagine a clock face with 60 minutes on it. Let the clock stand for the time men have had access to writing systems. Our clock would represent something like 3,000 years, and each minute on the clock 50 years. On this scale, there were no significant media changes until about 9 minutes ago. At that time, the printing press came into use in Western culture. About 3 minutes ago the telegraph, photograph, and locomotive arrived. 2 minutes ago: the telephone, rotary press, motion pictures, automobile, aeroplane, and radio. One minute ago, the talking-picture. TV has appeared in the last 10 seconds, the computer in the last 5, and communications satellites in the last second', N. Postman and C. Weingartner, *Teaching as a Subversive Activity* (1971).

- 'It was not until 1991 that the first articles by sociologists and psychologists discussing video games and their effects appeared. The impact of new forms of entertainment and education such as 'virtual reality' have yet to be felt. Sociologists of the media are always a long way behind the area they are investigating' – Andy Barnard and Terry Burgess, *Sociology Examined* (1996).

Advertising via the mass media plays a key role in the creation of a post-modern society. Such a society is 'characterised by style and images. We increasingly consume these images for their own sake. Style itself has become a commodity. This can be seen in the priority given to designer clothes and their identifying designer labels. And the media plays a central part in this process. Adverts sell images and style rather than content or substance' – P. Taylor *et al.*, *Sociology In Focus* (1996).

Technological change has transformed communication.

Electronic culture is displacing print culture.

2 | The effects of the media: theoretical approaches ▬▬

2.1 The media as 'hypodermic syringe'

- Ideas and beliefs are 'injected' into the minds of millions of people and transform the way they look at the world. Individuals are likened to 'empty buckets' into which ideologies and messages are filled.

- Totalitarian states are one-party dictatorships which use modern technology to indoctrinate entire populations in support of a single ideology. Nazi Germany and Stalinist Russia made systematic use of newspapers, radio, and cinema to spread official propaganda.

- The famous radio broadcast by Orson Welles in 1938 succeeded in persuading between 1–6 million Americans that the USA had been invaded by Martians.

- George Orwell's novel *Nineteen Eighty Four* (1949) refers to the emergence of a new media language – 'Newspeak' the 'only language in the world whose vocabulary gets smaller every year.' The aim of 'Newspeak' is to narrow the range of thought so that dissent becomes impossible: 'there will be no words in which to express it.' Mass culture theorists such as Marcuse see the media as having an Orwellian potential for manipulation.

2.2 'Uses and gratification' analysis

What people do with media rather than what media do with people.

- Individuals use the mass media for their own ends rather than being passive objects of manipulation. Viewers and readers actively interact with the media, and it is a mistake to see them as *tabula rasa* – a blank screen – soaking up whatever messages the media beam out.

- The media strengthen and reinforce existing opinions rather than changing them.

- The following concepts support the view that the media do not have a significant impact on beliefs and attitudes:

  - **Selective exposure:** individuals act as their own censors and only expose themselves to media material which fits in with their existing attitudes and interests

  - **Selective perception**: individuals 'read' their own prejudices and biases into what they see and read

  - **Selective retention:** individuals have selective memories and are likely to 'forget' media material which is unsympathetic to their viewpoints

- **The two-step flow of communication:** messages from the media have to win the support of **opinion leaders** if they are to be accepted by the mass of the population. Opinion leaders are individuals who exert a significant influence on those they meet informally. Although opinion leaders are not **opinion formers** (i.e. they do not hold formal media positions, such as newspaper editors or TV producers) they take a keen interest in media material and help shape the 'agenda' of discussion in everyday conversation.

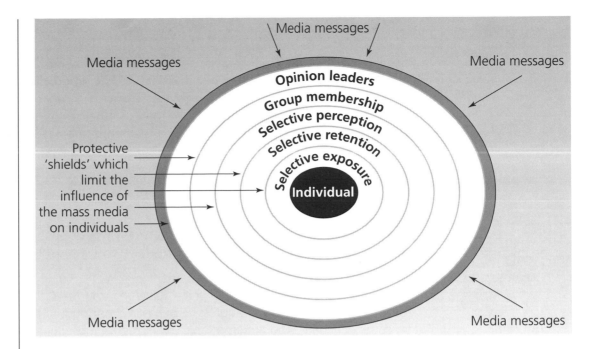

2.3 'Cultural effects' analysis

The gatekeeper function is a key sociological concept.

- The mass media exert a powerful influence, but not through crude indoctrination. Rather, they shape the 'frameworks of perception' – which individuals use to make sense of a highly complex world. Semiotic analysis reveals how specific ideological messages are 'encoded' in media texts i.e. TV programmes, films, books, newspapers, billboards etc. Greg Philos's research on the miners' strike of 1984–85 concluded that 'at least some of the information' which people use when they think about the world is derived from TV and newspapers, *Seeing and Believing* (1990).

- The media set the 'agenda' of public debate. The daily 'news' transmitted on television and printed in newspapers covers only a tiny fraction of the events which have actually taken place. The media's **gatekeeper** function determines what 'counts' as news. News items are ranked in order of priority, and presented from particular points of view.

- Society is 'a form of communication through which experience is described, shared, modified, and preserved...' Raymond Williams, *Communications* (1966). The power of the mass media flows from its capacity to alter society's understanding of itself.

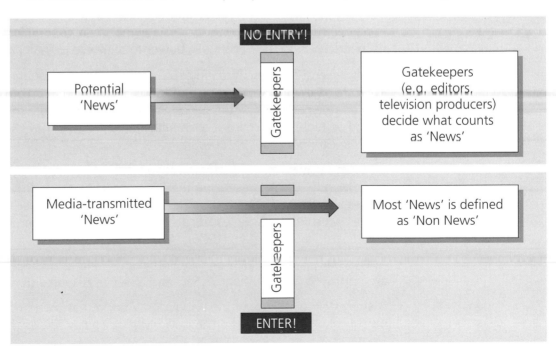

2.4 Media culture

- 'Media and consumer culture work hand in hand to generate thought and behaviour that conform to existing values, institutions, beliefs, and practices. Yet audiences may resist the dominant meanings and messages, create their own readings and appropriations of mass-produced culture, and use their culture as resources to empower themselves...' – Douglas Kellner, *Media Culture*, (1995).

3 The media and violence

> Problems in disentangling variables makes it difficult to reach firm conclusions.

- Violence (harm inflicted on living things) is widely portrayed in the media. By the age of 14 the average American boy or girl will have witnessed 11,000 murders on television.

- The classic study by Hilda Himmelweit – *Television and the Child* (1958) – concluded that 'TV is unlikely to cause aggressive behaviour, although it could precipitate it [in] those few children who are emotionally disturbed.' Subsequent research has overwhelmingly supported the view that it is an individual's family and social background – not the media programmes s/he is exposed to – which is the key factor in determining propensity for violent behaviour. However, in 1978 William Belson found that boys with high TV exposure had committed significantly more acts of violence than boys with low TV exposure.

- 'Heavy' TV viewers (4 hours or more each day) have been found to be more fearful than 'light' TV viewers because the former overestimate the level of violence and danger in society.

- Cultural effects theorists see exposure to media violence as undesirable because individuals may become desensitised to the consequences of violence. The influence of role-models on the young could lead them to see violence as a legitimate way of solving problems and over the long term the moral values of society might be corroded.

4 The media and gender

> Patriarchal ideology has weakened but is still evident.

- Men and women are portrayed in stereotyped ways. In advertisements women are usually featured as mothers, housewives or as sexual objects.

- Less than a quarter of the total staff employed in magazines and newspapers are female. Socialist feminists see the male owners and controllers of the media as deliberately using their economic power to reinforce patriarchal ideology.

- Marjorie Ferguson describes women's magazines as propagating a 'cult of femininity'. But in her view they are a source of 'positive self-esteem': 'For some women, there may be nowhere outside the pages of these journals where they are consistently valued so highly, or accorded such high status', *Forever Feminine: Women's Magazines and the Cult of Femininity* (1983).

- Children's comics reflect sharp gender divisions: 'Girls read "Bunty", "Judy", "June", and "Mandy" … all titles taking the form of a girl's name. Boys read comics with names like "Victor", "Valiant", "Hotspur", "Lion", "Thunder", and "Hornet" – names which embody virile masculine associations.' Sue Sharpe, *Just Like a Girl. How Girls Learn To Be Women*, (1976).

- Analysis of fairy tales such as 'Sleeping Beauty' and 'Cinderella' shows how females are portrayed as dependent victims and males as resourceful problem-solvers.

- A study of the 'politics of the living room' found that the remote control device was most likely to be in male hands. David Morley, *Family Television: Cultural Power and Domestic Power*, (1986).

- Media images of gender are not fixed, but reflect cultural change. Angela McRobbie believes there is now more 'fluidity' about what femininity means and an 'unfixing' has taken place in the roles ascribed to young women, *Postmodernism and Popular Culture* (1994).

5 | The media and ethnicity

Racist ideology has weakened but is still evident.

- Black people have been portrayed in negative and stereotyped ways by the mass media. Stuart Hall *et al*'s study – *Policing the Crisis* (1979) showed how the crime of 'mugging' was overwhelmingly presented as a 'black' crime.

- An analysis of the reporting of ethnic issues in 1985 and 1989 by Van Dijk found that the press (especially the tabloids) portrayed black people as a 'problem' and a 'threat' to mainstream society, *Racism and the Press* (1991).

- The crude racial stereotyping common on TV in the 1950s and 1960s has faded, but individuals from ethnic minority backgrounds continue to be under-represented in 'success' roles. 'Most young black males on TV are fast-talking hustlers living on the edge of the law, or crack dealers in flashy cars ... Black characters are on the periphery of an all-white cast or feature in "their own" all-black programmes, such as "Desmonds" and "The Cosby Show" –Barnard and Burgess, *Sociology Explained* (1996).

- **Uses and gratification theorists** see the media as marginally reinforcing existing attitudes and beliefs on race. **Cultural effects theorists** see the media as playing an important role in disseminating either racist or non-racist values.

6 | The media and political bias

6.1 Television

Pluralist view:

Pluralists see the media as providing many points of view.

- Television gives an impartial coverage of political issues. Television journalists are trained to be 'biased against bias' and to report both sides of controversial debates. The **pluralist model** (which is similar to a functionalist view) sees the media as reflecting the public consensus on values and beliefs.

- Hundreds of people with very different social backgrounds and political affiliations are involved in the production of news and political programmes. The 1954 Television Act states that programmes should 'maintain a proper balance in their subject matter.'

- If a news item is judged to be 'newsworthy' (i.e. important and significant for people in Britain) it will be included in the news. Such judgements are made on professional and not on ideological grounds.

Anti-pluralist view:

Anti-pluralists see the media as providing the ideologically dominant point of view.

- Television fails to give an impartial coverage of political issues. Glasgow University Media Group argues that television news coverage reflects a London-based, white middle-class liberal consensus. Both the BBC and ITN give a 'pro-establishment' interpretation of events. Bias is reflected in the use of language (e.g. employers make 'offers' while trade unions make 'threats').

- Television coverage of the 1985/86 miners' strike was dominated by the ideologically loaded themes of 'violence against working miners', and the 'drift back to work'.

- The Media Monitoring Unit set up by Lord Tebbit also saw television as being ideologically biased – but against the right rather than the left. The BBC was staffed by 'liberal-leftists' who selectively edited programmes and slanted the news in a way which marginalised right-wing political viewpoints.

- Anti-pluralists support either a **mass manipulative model** of the media (i.e. the media is deliberately used as a mechanism of ideological indoctrination) or a **hegemonic model** (i.e. media messages reflect the dominant ideological consensus).

6.2 Newspapers

Pluralist view:

- A high proportion of readers ignore the political content of newspapers and concentrate on sport, photographs, television schedules, etc.

- Many readers vote against the political advice of their newspaper. One study found that 25% of readers of *The Sun* did not know which political party it supported.

- The bias of the press is counter-balanced by politically neutral radio and television. Seventy per cent of the public say that TV news is their most important source of information on politics.

- In the 1997 General Election the majority of newspapers advised their readers to support the Labour Party, thus refuting the claim that the press is permanently biased in favour of the Conservative Party.

Anti-pluralist view:

- Voting patterns tend to match choice of newspaper (e.g. most *Mirror* readers vote Labour and most *Telegraph* readers vote Conservative).

- Polls show that newspapers are the second most important source of information about politics (after television), so their political influence cannot be ignored.

- William Miller found that tabloid newspapers were likely to influence the voting of their politically uncommitted readers, *Media and Voters* (1991).

  There is a high degree of interchange between television and newspaper journalists, and the 'news' items they select are very similar, Patrick Dunleavy, *The Influence of the Press* (1987).

- The 1992 General Election was far more typical of post-war elections than 1997. In 1992 70% of the readers of daily newspapers, and 62% of the readers of Sunday newspapers, were urged to vote Conservative.

7 | Control of the media

7.1 Pluralist view:

- The media are ultimately controlled by the people. If the public's tastes and preferences are ignored sales / viewing ratings will fall. Only those media organisations attuned to their customers' interests will be profitable.

- John Whale describes how from 1964 to 1969 *The Sun* newspaper 'struggled to interest working people principally through the intellect. The paper had declined inexorably. Murdoch gave up the attempt and went for baser instincts. Sales soared', *The Politics of the Media* (1977). Readers, in other words, get what they want.

- The range of television and radio programmes, newspapers and magazines, films and videos available in Britain shows that a wide variety of tastes and interests are met. If significant potential demand existed for a media product that was not available on the market (e.g. a new left-wing or right-wing daily newspaper) then an investor would come forward, create it, and make profits from it.

- Although most national newspapers have been pro-Conservative this has not prevented the Labour Party from winning seven general elections since 1945.

Right-wing individuals believe the media is biased against right-wing viewpoints.

Left-wing individuals believe the media is biased against left-wing viewpoints.

Pluralists believe that the market expresses the popular consensus.

- The state imposes some restrictions on the media but this is essential in any democratic society in order to safeguard national security. In a totalitarian society the state systematically monitors and censors all expressions of opinion. In Britain the media act as the 'watchdog of the constitution' and play a vital role in scrutinising government actions and safeguarding individual liberties.

7.2 Anti-pluralist view:

- The ownership of the media has been concentrated in fewer and fewer hands. Conglomerates (large companies with a wide range of business interests) have become increasingly powerful, and the number of daily national newspapers has continued to decline – from 14 in 1921 to 10 today. Rupert Murdoch owns (amongst other global media) *The Times*, the *Sunday Times*, the *News of the World*, *The Sun*, BSkyB satellite television, HarperCollins publishers, Twentieth Century Fox.

- Owners of newspapers have sacked editors who stepped politically out of line. A journalist on *The Times* who wrote an article which was critical of the owner of the paper found it was withdrawn from publication.

- The majority of journalists practise self-censorship in order to keep their jobs. When Victor Matthews took over the *Daily Express* he declared: 'By and large editors will have complete freedom as long as they agree with the policy I have laid down.'

- Around two-thirds of newspaper income comes from advertisers, and fear of losing advertising revenue may inhibit criticism of advertisers' companies.

- The distribution of newspapers and magazines is controlled by three companies, and some publications have been refused distribution.

- The state can exert pressure on the media, e.g. the Director-General of the BBC and members of its board of governors are appointed by the Government. If the BBC is too critical of government policy the licence fee (the main source of the BBC's revenue) can be 'frozen'. Since 1912 D-Notices (Defence Notices) have been issued which 'advise' editors not to make certain items of information public. Under the 1989 Official Secrets Act it is an offence for a government employee to 'leak' information to the media.

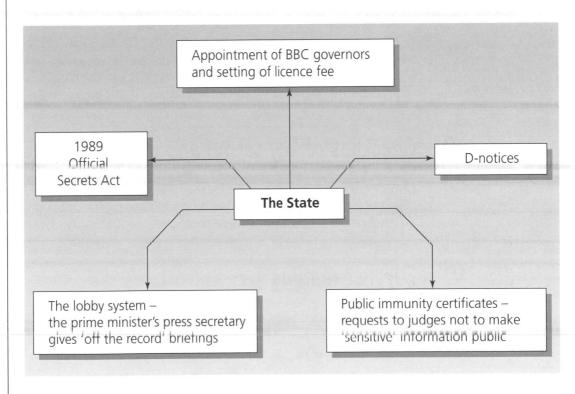

8 | Key studies

McLuhan coined the term 'global village'.

- *Understanding Media: The Extensions of Man* (1964), Marshall McLuhan. Divides the history of the development of communications into three main stages: 1) Prior to the invention of printing in the 15th century the main medium was speech – direct face-to-face interaction. 2) Printing transformed communication. Reading and writing (solitary and isolated activities) made for non-involvement. 3) With the birth of the electronic media of radio and TV the world becomes a 'global village'. News travels instantaneously from place to place and this makes for increased involvement across national and class boundaries.

- *Television in Politics: Its Uses And Influence* (1968), J. G. Blumer and D. McQuail, found that television political broadcasts reinforced rather than changed viewers' political beliefs. People became more informed about party policies, but there was little change in voting intentions. The individuals who were the most likely to be influenced by broadcasts were those who lacked strong political convictions. The Liberal Party gained most support from this group.

- *The Selling of the President 1968* (1970) by Joe McGinniss. From 1952 on advertising agencies began to 'sell' Presidents to voters. Image – not policies and issues – have dominated election campaigns. Nixon failed in 1960 because of the image the viewers received... 'It's not what's *there* that counts, its what's projected.'

The Glasgow University Media Group carried out pioneering research on ideology in the media.

- *Bad News, the Glasgow University Media Group* (1976). Television news broadcasts are ideologically biased and certain individuals and institutions are favoured. Moreover, 'the picture of society in general and industrial society in particular' that is constructed puts the 'blame for society's industrial and economic problems at the door of the workforce.' In *Really Bad News* (1982) a study of TV news found that 'In the 13 weeks of the Glasgow dustcart drivers' strike, which was reported in 102 bulletins and included 20 interviews, not once did a striker get to state his case nationally in an interview.'

- *Political Communications* by Kenneth Newton in *The Developing British Political System: the 1990s* (1993) eds I. Budge and D. McKay. The 1980s were 'unusually restrictive...(with) the arrest and trial of the civil servants, Clive Ponting and Sarah Tisdale, for leaking documents; a long series of controversies about TV programmes and attempts to censor them; the attempt to prevent the publication of 'Spycatcher', the memoirs of a secret service agent, Peter Wright; the admission that M15 vetted BBC journalists; a dossier submitted by the Conservative party chairman, Norman Tebbit, alleging BBC news bias, especially on the American bombing of Libya; the banning of a TV programme on Zircon (a spy satellite) and subsequent Special Branch raids on the homes and offices of journalists and broadcasters...'

9 | Checklist of key terms and concepts

Mass media   Totalitarian   *Tabula rasa*   Selective exposure   Selective perception
Selective retention   Two-step flow of communication   Opinion leader   Opinion former
Gatekeeper function   Agenda-setting function   Cathartic   Conglomerates

10 | Further reading

Eldridge, J. (ed.) (1993) *Getting the Message: News, Truth and Power*, London, Routledge.

Trowler, P. (1996) *Investigating Mass Media* (2nd edition), London, Collins Educational.

Tunstall, J. (1983) *The Media in Britain*, London, Constable.

Van Zoonen, L. (1994) *Feminist Media Studies*, London, Sage.

Chapter seven

Families

1 | Definitions

- The family is a *kinship group*, 'a group of persons directly linked by kin connections, the adult members of which assume responsibility for caring for children', Anthony Giddens, *Sociology* (1997). Kinship connections are based on blood, marriage, or adoption.

- *Marriage:* a socially recognised union between two adults.

- *Monogamy:* a man or woman being married to one individual at a time.

- *Serial Monogamy:* individuals have a succession of monogamous relationships.

- *Polygamy:* a man or woman is able to marry more than one spouse. This can take the form of *polyandry* (a woman is married to more than one husband at the same time) or – more commonly – *polygyny* (a husband is married to more than one wife at the same time).

1.1 Types of family

- *Nuclear families:* spouses (husband and wife) live with their children in the same residence. (Sometimes described as the 'cereal packet family'.) A quarter of households in the UK consist of a married couple and their dependent children.

- *Extended families:* two or more generations either live together in the same household or see each other on a regular (e.g. daily) basis.

- *One-parent families* (sometimes known as *single-parent or lone-parent families*): 22% of families with children are headed by lone parents – nearly three times the proportion in 1971. This increase has resulted from the rise in the divorce rate (around 40% of marriages end in divorce) and in the number of births outside marriage (34% of babies are born to unmarried mothers, compared with 8% in 1971).

- *Reconstituted families* (sometimes known as step-families since at least one of the adults is a step-parent): divorce, or the death of a spouse, can lead to a new family being formed. One or both partners bring children from past relationships to the new family.

- *Same-sex families:* these are formed, for example, by a woman leaving her husband, taking her children, and going to live with another woman.

1.2 Households, families and social policy

- Some sociologists favour the term **households** rather than **families**. The term household refers to the residence or living space of individuals (or one individual) who share facilities and have a 'common cooking-pot' (i.e. they take meals together). Some households are based on families (individuals with kin connections), some households are not (e.g. a group of students who share a house).

- David Morgan points out that all families are subject to constant change and fluidity. 'Family members grow older and move in and out of different households through death, marriage, birth, divorce or simply leaving home.' Family life has to be viewed as a process, 'as a set of practices rather than as a structure of relatively fixed roles and expectations', 'Thinking About Family Life', *Sociology Review*, April 1998.

Family structure has become more diverse.

Is 'household' less ideological than 'family'?

- **Social policy** refers to the intervention of central and local government in the lives of individuals and communities. The state attempts to encourage those forms of family life which are seen as 'normal' and discourage those which are seen as 'deviant'. Changes in ideology result in changes in social policy, (e.g. at some times governments have thought it desirable to provide extra financial assistance to lone-parent families while at other times such assistance has been withdrawn).

2 | Theoretical perspectives

2.1 Functionalist

Functionalists celebrate the nuclear family.

- The family performs a number of functions vital for the survival of a social system. These include reproduction, socialisation (the inculcation of core values and norms), maintenance (the care of the dependent young), and the affective function (meeting of emotional needs for affection).

- G.H. Murdock studied 250 different societies and concluded that the family was 'universal', i.e. found in all societies. One apparent exception is the Israeli kibbutz, but in the functionalist view the entire kibbutz operates as an extended family.

- Kingsley Davis believes the family performs a number of key functions including placement (i.e. assigning individuals to occupations).

- Talcott Parsons viewed the two core functions of the family as being socialisation of children and the stabilisation of adult personalities.

- Parsons sees the nuclear family as ideally suited to modern industrial society. It is a compact and geographically mobile unit, not tied to the kinship ties of a particular locality, and consequently able to respond to the ever-changing demands of the labour market.

- Critics see functionalists as giving a one-sided 'happy families' picture of family life. The family is more 'functional' for men than for women (who do most of the housework and child care).

2.2 Marxist

- The classic Marxist analysis was set out by Friedrich Engels in 1884 and made use of research carried out by the American anthropologist L.H. Morgan (1818–81). Morgan believed that men and women originally had the same status, but with the break up of tribal society women became the 'property' of husbands. Thus the emergence of a class-divided society was accompanied by the establishment of the patriarchal monogamous family. Engels claimed that the modern family was 'founded on the open or concealed domestic slavery of the wife... Within the family he (the husband) is the bourgeois, and the wife represents the proletariat.'

Marxists see families as functional to Capitalism.

- Engels argued that 'the emancipation of woman will only be possible when woman can take part in production on a large, social scale, and domestic work no longer claims anything but an insignificant amount of her time.' Private housekeeping had to be 'transformed into a social industry.' In the early 1920s the revolutionary Alexandra Kollantai attempted to implement some of Engels' ideas in the Soviet Union.

- According to neo-Marxist analysis the domestic labour performed by women contributes to the profitability of capitalism. Wage-earners are 'serviced' free of charge and kept in productive condition. Women also act as a 'reserve army' of labour, a source of part-time / casual labour when this is required by the labour market. The purchase of consumer goods by families is an important source of profit for business. The accumulation of debt (or 'credit') intensifies pressure on adult family members to work hard and obey their employers.

- Reproducing children is functional for capitalism since it provides the capitalists of tomorrow with a new generation of workers to exploit.

- Critics view Marxist analysis as mechanical and reductionist. It has an 'over-socialised' view of individuals as passively accepting their position in the class structure. The changing patterns of family life are ignored as is the possibility that gender inequality is rooted in patriarchal attitudes rather than class divisions.

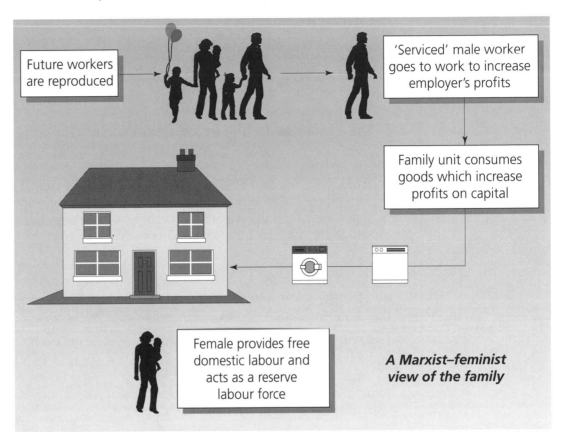

Future workers are reproduced

'Serviced' male worker goes to work to increase employer's profits

Family unit consumes goods which increase profits on capital

Female provides free domestic labour and acts as a reserve labour force

A Marxist–feminist view of the family

2.3 The Action theory / Interpretive view

- In contrast to the **macro** (large-scale structural) approach of functionalists and Marxists, interpretivists use a **micro** (small-scale meanings-focused) approach.

- Peter Berger and Hansfried Kellner analysed marriage as **a social construction**, a shared narrative (or story) which has to be created and sustained, *Approaches to the History of the Western Family* (1980). 'Marriage in our society is a dramatic act in which two strangers come together and re-define themselves.' Shared rituals (such as birthdays and anniversaries) help reinforce this 'imagined' family identity.

- Radical psychiatry uses an interactionist approach to show how the dynamics of family life can result in mental illness. Some parents seek to over-control their children, and threats of withdrawal of love are used as a form of 'psychic terrorism' to keep children in line, R.D. Laing, *Sanity, Madness and the Family* (1970).

- It is a mistake to reify families and see them as 'machines' or 'institutions'. Families are the outcomes of the interpretations made by interacting individuals and as such are inherently precarious.

- Critics of social action / interpretive analysis note that it ignores the structural (macro) influences on family life. It fails 'to handle, systematically, the wider sets of relationships within which the family is placed', D.H.J. Morgan, *Social Theory and the Family* (1975).

Action theorists reject structural explanations of the family.

3 | Debates on the family

3.1 The nuclear family in pre-industrial society

The nuclear family is not new.

- According to functionalists, just as the needs of industrial society are met by the isolated and mobile nuclear family so the needs of pre-industrial society were met by the immobile extended family.

- However, historical research on family life in 17th century England by Peter Laslett shows that the nuclear family, not the extended family, was the norm and that considerable geographical mobility existed. *The World We Have Lost* (1965).

3.2 The extended family in industrial society

- Functionalists view the nuclear family as the dominant form of family life in industrial societies. Thus Norman Bell and Ezra Vogel argue that industrialisation leads to increased physical movement from one locality to another, and decreased contact between kin. Since achievement is recognised more than birth kin have less to offer an individual in return for his / her submission, *A Modern Introduction to the Family* (1960).

- Critics of functionalist analysis point out that it gives insufficient recognition to non-nuclear family forms. A study of Preston in 1851 found that the extended family was dominant and functioned as a 'mini-welfare state'.

- From the mid-1950s the extended family was 're-discovered' in working-class communities such as Bethnal Green and Hull. A study in Swansea found no evidence to support the view that the family had been 'stripped bare' of its kinship ties. The term 'dispersed extended family' is used to emphasise how families keep in touch with relatives through visits and the telephone.

3.3 The symmetrical family

Is domestic labour still a female preserve?

- In *The Symmetrical Family* (1975) Young and Wilmott put forward the view that relationships between husbands and wives are far more balanced and egalitarian than in the past, with household chores and child care being increasingly shared. Earlier studies of working-class families had found conjugal (marriage) roles to be highly segregated. In contrast, the study by Young and Willmott revealed that 72% of husbands regularly helped with the housework.

Is housework still housewife work?

- However Ann Oakley in *The Sociology of Housework* (1974) found no evidence to support the view that the family was becoming 'symmetrical'. Only in 15% of the small number of families she studied did men have a high level of participation in housework. Research by Jonathan Gershuny shows that – although there has been a modest shift towards a 'symmetrical' pattern – the main burden of domestic work continues to be carried by women.

3.4 The instability of family life

- Edward Shorter gives a positive account of the family: 'Warm and sheltering, the nuclear family kept the children secure from the pressure of the outside adult world, and gave the men an evening refuge from the icy blast of competition', *The Making of the Modern Family* (1976). However, he points out that the family is essentially unstable since it is based on sexual attraction between husband and wife (rather than, for example, on pre-arranged property transactions).

- Edmund Leach focuses on the limited support nuclear families receive from kin and neighbours. The domestic household today 'is isolated. The family looks inward upon itself; there is an intensification of emotional stress between husband and wife, and parents and children. The strain is greater than most of us can bear' – 'A Runaway World?', *Reith Lectures* (1967). Manifestations of this 'strain' include domestic violence (over 80% of homicides of women have a 'domestic' context), rape within marriage (still legal until 1991), and child abuse.

- The American sociologist Urie Brofenbrenner believes the pressures of work and consumerism have led to a reduction in the amount of 'quality' emotional time that parents spend with their children. Children have been the main casualties of the changes in family life over recent decades.

- Alvin Toffler notes that men and women 'are often torn in conflict between a commitment to career and a commitment to children.' He speculates that 'in the future, many couples will side-step this problem by deferring the entire task of raising children after retirement...', *Future Shock* (1971). (Toffler believes people should retire early and can remain fit into their sixties.)

3.5 The New Right critique of the family

- American writer Charles Murray was brought to Britain by the *The Sunday Times* to investigate whether 'this country was developing an American-style underclass.'

- Murray's analysis of the 'statistical state of the British family' published in 1994 focused on the increase in illegitimacy (from 9.2% in 1976 to almost one in three in the early 1990s); co-habitation (in 1991 6% of families were headed by a cohabiting couple); and divorce (three times higher in the 1990s compared with the 1960s).

- Murray argued that the two-parent family was ceasing to be the norm, thus causing a collapse in the 'civilising process' and young males becoming an unsocialised 'rabble'.

- His 'minimalist solution' in terms of social policy changes is to 'stop making the benefit system favour single mothers over married mothers.'

- A number of 'ethical socialists' have been sympathetic to aspects of Murray's analysis. A.H. Halsey writes that children in one-parent families 'tend to die earlier, to have more illness, to do less well at school, to exist at a lower level of nutrition, comfort and conviviality, to suffer more unemployment, to be more prone to deviance and crime, and finally to repeat the cycle of unstable parenting from which they themselves have suffered.' Norman Dennis criticises the 'intelligentsia in higher education' for ignoring 'the disappearance of the responsible father' and for popularising the complacent slogan that 'the family is not deteriorating, only changing.' *Times Higher Education Supplement* (29.10.93).

- Critics claim that Murray puts forward a romanticised picture of the traditional two-parent family; is historically superficial (rates of illegitimacy, co-habitation, and family breakdown have been high in the past); ignores the 'dark side' of conventional nuclear family life (including violence against women); implicitly seeks to confine women to a housework / child care role; and fails to point to any positive opportunities provided by the emergence of a less stereotyped pattern of family life.

Ethical socialists agree with the New Right.

Was there ever a 'golden age' of the family?

4 | Divorce and the decline of marriage

- The divorce rate (the number of divorces in a given year divided by the number of marriages), the number of divorce petitions (requests for divorce), and the number of divorce absolutes (final legally terminated divorces) have risen dramatically. During this century the number of divorce absolutes granted has increased more than two hundred times.

- Marriage has declined and according to *Social Trends* (Vol. 27 1997) in twenty years' time less than half the adult population will be married. More than one in three children are now born outside marriage.

- Cohabiting has increased: in 1995 one in four women aged 14 to 29 who were single, widowed, divorced or separated were cohabiting.

- Average size of households has declined from 4.6 persons per household in 1900 to 2.4 in 1996. In 1996 28% of all households consisted of people living on their own.

4.1 Factors which have led to the rise in divorce

- **Legal changes:** the 1969 Divorce Reform Act made it possible to end a marriage on the grounds of 'irretrievable breakdown' (rather than proving guilt). Until 1937 adultery was the only type of offence legally recognised as warranting the dissolution of the marriage relationship. Until 1857 a private Act of Parliament had to be passed. (The average number of divorces in the period 1851–55 was four.)

- **The changing status of women:** 70% of divorce petitions are initiated by women. Increased economic independence enables women to opt out of an emotionally unfulfilling relationship. The pressures of women's 'triple shift' – housework, paid employment, and provision of emotional support – can lead to marriage breakdown.

- **Demographic factors:** when life-expectancy was low, marriages were ended by death. In the 1960s and 1970s there was a trend towards marrying at an earlier age, and early marriages (especially in cases of pre-marital pregnancy) were associated with a greater risk of divorce.

- **New social values:** the stigma of divorce has lessened, the influence of religious ideas has declined, cohabitation has become more common.

- **More isolated and privatised families:** increased geographical mobility, the weakening of kinship ties, and the decline in support from relatives has made husbands and wives increasingly dependent on each other for affective support – and there is little to hold a marriage together if a couple lose their emotional rapport for each other.

- **Problems of inter-personal communication:** partners who are from different class / ethnic / religious / cultural backgrounds or ages are more prone to divorce.

5 | Is the nuclear family still the norm?

No:

- R. Rapoport (editor of *Families in Britain* (1982)) writes: 'The stereotype of family group consisting of father, mother, and at least two residing children is entirely misleading. A majority of households now consist of solitaries, couples without offspring, or single-parent households', *Families in Britain* (1982).

- The increasingly diverse pattern of family life now includes: **dual-worker** families (where both husbands and wives are in paid employment); **one-parent families** (22% of families with children); **reconstituted families** (in over 30% of divorces both partners remarry); **extended** families (common in the Asian community); and **communes** (the numbers of which increased in the 1970s).

Yes:

- Robert Chester points out that although divorce rates have risen and the diversity of family styles has increased, the 'family based on a married couple living with their children, and committed to a permanent relationship, is still the norm.'

- The majority of people will continue to spend most of their lives in a family environment and 'place a high value on it.' The majority of the divorced remarry.

- The increase in one-parent families should not obscure the fact that nearly four-fifths of children continue to live with their natural parents.

- In the nineteenth century proportionately more children were affected by marital disruption (because of the death of a parent) than are affected by divorce today.

- Cohabitation is often a transitional and temporary phase prior to marriage. The continuities in family life in Britain are in fact more striking than the discontinuities – 'The Rise of the Neo-Conventional family', *New Society*, 9 May 1985.

6 | Checklist of key terms and concepts

Monogamy Serial monogamy Polygamy Polyandry Nuclear family Extended family Household Reconstituted family Dual-worker family Reserve army of labour Modified extended family Dispersed extended family Symmetrical family Conjugal roles Divorce petitions Divorce absolutes Divorce rate.

7 | Further reading

Barrett, M. and McIntosh, M. (1982) *The Anti-Social Family*, London, Verso.

Gittens, D. (1993) *The Family in Question*, 2nd edition, London, Macmillan.

Jorgensen, N. (1995) *Investigating Families and Households*, London, Collins Educational.

Morgan, D. (1985) *The Family, Politics and Social Theory*, London, Routledge.

Chapter eight

Gender

1 Definition

Examiners expect you to distinguish between sex and gender.

- **Sex:** biological/anatomical differences between males and females.
- **Gender:** social and cultural identities which are assigned to males and females.

2 Theoretical explanations of gender differences

2.1 Biology is destiny

- Gender inequalities are viewed as direct reflections of biological inequalities. Because of their respective body chemicals and hormones, women are 'naturally' more passive and dependent and have a 'maternal instinct'. And men are 'naturally' more assertive than women.

- L. Tiger and R. Fox believe that males and females are genetically programmed to behave in different ways since they do not share the same **biogrammar**, *The Imperial Animal* (1972).

- A. Moir and D. Jessel believe that the structure of the male brain differs from the structure of the female's. Males are better at mathematics because the male brain has superior spatial ability while females are better at language because the female brain is more sensitive to sound, *BrainSex: The Real Differences Between Men and Women* (1989).

- Sociobiologists believe that human behaviour is genetically determined. Males are driven by instincts to seek to impregnate as many females as possible. Females are programmed to be more selective in their choice of sexual partners.

2.2 Functionalist theory and role specialisation

Role-specialisation is a key functionalist concept.

- Talcott Parsons believes that gender roles are shaped by both biological and cultural factors. Biological differences predispose women to specialise in **expressive roles** (i.e. expressing emotions and dealing with relationships), and men to specialise in **instrumental roles** (i.e. earning money in paid employment).

- What culture does is to 'work with the grain' of biology. Women are best suited to caring for children. As they are the ones who give birth, and thus experience a close emotional bond with the baby. Cultural differences in gender socialisation are built on the pre-existing bedrock of biological differences.

2.3 Neo-Marxist theory and women as an exploited class

- Neo-Marxists see domestic labour as a key factor behind women's subordinate role in modern society. Women service and maintain the labour force and reproduce the next generation of workers from which profits will be extracted.

- According to an estimate made by the Office for National Statistics (October 1997) domestic labour is worth £739 billion a year to the British economy. In Sheila Rowbotham's view capitalism is as 'dependent on women's work in the home as on the exploitation of labour outside', *Women, Resistance and Revolution* (1972). Women's subordination comes from their exploitation as an unpaid, marginalised, houseworking / child-caring proletariat.

2.4 Feminist theory – men like things as they are

- **Gender inequalities are a direct product of patriarchy.** 'Private patriarchy is based upon household production, with a patriarch controlling women individually and directly in the relatively private sphere of the home. Public patriarchy is based on structures other than the household...', Sylvia Walby, *Theorising Patriarchy* (1990).

- **Men have a vested interest in the status quo.** They dominate almost all positions of power, receive more pay than women, hold the majority of high status jobs, and make the least contribution to unpaid labour (i.e. housework, child-care, etc.).

- **Men dominate important social institutions such as pubs.** 'The male ability to command and control a space seems to be one of the first lessons of social learning', Valerie Hey, *Patriarchy and Pub Culture* (1986).

- **Existentialist feminists** like Simone de Beauvoir believe that women must change themselves, become more assertive and intellectually competent, and play a more active role in the public sphere (e.g. become MPs) if gender inequalities are to be confronted.

- **Liberal feminism:** equality between men and women can be achieved through a gradual step-by-step process of reform which removes forms of discrimination and barriers to equal rights (e.g. the passing of the 1970 Equal Pay Act and the 1975 Sex Discrimination Act).

- **Marxist and socialist feminism:** women form a 'sex-class' – the most exploited section of the working class. Capitalism divided the workforce into 'wage earners and those dependent upon the wage of others', M. Barrett, *Women's Oppression Today* (1980).

- **Radical feminism:** patriarchy (male domination) rather than class is the fundamental cause of women's oppression. Problems of rape, pornography, sexual harassment, and male violence towards women will not automatically disappear under a new mode of production. The roots of female subordination are ideological rather than economic.

- **Black feminism:** white feminists have been criticised for seeing all women (the 'sisterhood') as being in the same boat. But the problems faced by middle-class white women are very different from those faced by poorer women in minority communities, who are confronted by the 'triple disadvantages' of racism, sexism, and poverty.

- **Post-feminism:** also focuses on the diversity of women's experience. 'The term "woman" is seen as having no single meaning as women's identity has become increasingly fragmented (e.g. black women, lesbian women, working-class women). There is agreement with post-modernism that large-scale theorising is no longer valid', A.Barnard and T. Burgess, *Sociology Explained* (1996).

- **Post-modern feminism:** Carol Gilligan believes that women have more caring and altruistic attitudes than men. Instead of women striving to become 'more like men' (i.e. treating people in an instrumental way and seeking more power and status) men should strive to become more like women (i.e. become 'The New Man'). Women should recognise the positive attributes of their own gender socialisation.

Patriarchy is a key sociological concept.

Radical feminists see men as the problem. Socialist feminists see capitalism as the problem.

3 | Women and work

- Pat Mayes, *Gender* (1986) notes that:

  1 Female occupations reflect female domestic roles – the majority of cleaners, cooks, infant teachers, and nurses are female;

  2 Females predominate in occupations which require deferential behaviour such as waitressing and shop-work;

  3 Many females perform a double-shift – in addition to their paid employment they carry out domestic responsibilities (such as cooking the evening meal).

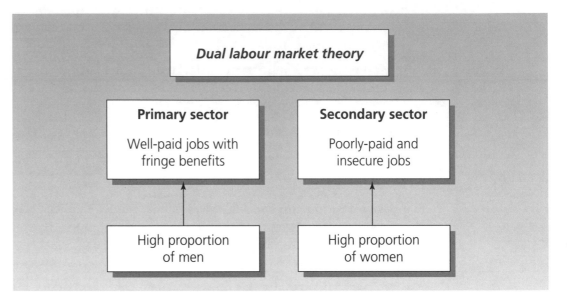

- According to **dual labour market theory** a high proportion of women work in the secondary sector (characterised by jobs which are low-paid, insecure, with poor promotion prospects). A high proportion of men work in the primary sector (characterised by jobs which are well-paid, secure, with fringe benefits. etc.).

You must know your dual labour market theory!

- **Horizontal segregation** exists when men and women are concentrated in different occupations. (e.g. men in fishing, mining, agriculture, women in social work, and personal services such as hairdressing). **Vertical segregation** exists when men and women are concentrated in different status levels within the same institution / sector (e.g. in most further education colleges the senior management team is male-dominated while the cleaning staff is female-dominated).

- Women make up 32% of all full-time workers.

- Women are under-represented on the boards of directors of top companies (fewer than 1 in 20 is female), and in the upper reaches of management. 'Glass-ceilings' and 'old boy networks' block women's ascent into the most highly paid and influential positions.

- The majority of part-time jobs are carried out by women. 84% of part-time employees are women. Most housework (especially the 'hard' chores of cooking, cleaning and child-care) is carried out by women. In her pioneering research Ann Oakley argued that housework is defined as 'non-work' rather than 'real' work, and yet the average housewife 'spends between 3,000 and 4,000 hours a year on housework', *Housewife* (1976).

Is there a genderquake or just a faint gendertremor?

- The Demos think-tank sees historic changes taking place in the relationships between men and women in the under 35 age group constituting a **genderquake**. Women's aspirations have changed (a career is a higher priority than children, with the average age for women having their first child now nearly 28); the majority of new jobs created over the last twenty years have gone to women; women's average earnings have increased more rapidly than men's; there has been a sharp increase in women's representation in the professions, Helen Wilkinson, *No Turning Back: Generations and the Genderquake* (1994). A 1995 Demos study detects a profound shift: 'male' manual jobs are disappearing; females are outperforming males in education (a majority of university students are now female); men's values are being 'feminised' and 'a swing away from traditional masculinity' is evident.

- The number of female MPs has risen from 1 in 1918 to 120 in 1997. (However, over four-fifths of MPs are still male.)

- Catherine Hakim describes how 'On the one hand women are concentrated in the lowest grade, least skilled and lowest paid jobs with the poorest employment benefits and prospects. On the other hand women report high levels of satisfaction with their jobs...' This paradox can be explained by women 'having different life goals from men. Most women's preference has been for the home-maker role, with paid employment regarded as a secondary activity, to be fitted in as and when the home-maker activities allow it...', 'Grateful Slaves and Self-made Women: Fact and Fantasy in Women's Work Orientations', *The European Sociological Review*, vol. 7, no.2, 1991.

- Critics of Hakim argue that structural pressures and limited opportunities rather than different 'life goal choices', shape the pattern of women's participation in the labour force.

4 | Men

The study of men as gendered beings has focused on:

The study of 'gender' often ignores men!

- **The social construction of masculinity: masculinism** is 'the ideology that justifies and naturalises male domination. Masculinism takes it for granted that there is a fundamental difference between men and women, it assumes that heterosexuality is normal, it accepts without question the sexual division of labour, and it sanctions the political and dominant role of men in the public and private spheres', Arthur Brittan, *Masculinity and Power* (1989).

- **The crisis of masculinity:** the decline in manual jobs and the growth in male unemployment has made it more difficult to sustain the traditional male 'breadwinner' role. Rising suicide rates amongst young males have been related to increased uncertainty about the nature of masculine identity.

- **Men's movements:** K. Clatterbaugh in *Contemporary Perspectives On Masculinity* (1990) lists the following perspectives on masculinity.

- **Conservative:** 'biological conservatives' view patriarchy as rooted in genetics and evolution; 'moral conservatives' see men as 'barbarians' who can only be civilised by being made to conform to traditional male roles.

- **Profeminist:** 'radical profeminists' are highly critical of male behaviour, while 'liberal profeminists' see both men and women as victims of the existing pattern of gender socialisation (e.g. men are also victims of male violence).

- **Men's rights:** men, not women, are the oppressed gender (e.g. some divorced men have to leave their home, lose custody of children, and pay maintenance, even though they were not the 'unfaithful' partner).

- **Socialist:** masculinity is an example of an 'alienated' identity, a product of the de-humanisation of life in capitalism.

- **Spiritual searchers:** men have lost touch with the 'wild' side of their natures and need to gain a deeper understanding of their drives and needs.

- **Group-specific:** different groups of men have different problems and experiences (e.g. homosexual men, like women, are also the victims of patriarchy).

5 | Can a gender-neutral society be established?

No:

- In the view of sociobiologists differences in gender roles are based on genetics and evolution. Each sex has been programmed to follow different strategies for mating, reproduction, etc.

- Functionalists believe that the existing division of labour in child-care will continue since females perform expressive roles with greater competence than males.

- Some feminists claim that patriarchal attitudes are too deeply embedded in men's psyches for them to be able to share power and make an equal contribution to the domestic mode of production.

Yes:

- Explanations of inequalities in terms of genetics and evolution are based on 'biological reductionism'. They ignore the ways in which gender identities are socially constructed. Cross-cultural research shows that in some societies males perform 'feminine' roles and females perform 'masculine' roles.

- If behaviour is 'fixed' by biology how are the dramatic changes in gender roles which have taken place over the last century to be explained?

- Patriarchal attitudes are in decline, but women as well as men will have to change. In the view of Ros Coward most women 'comply with traditional structures and expectations, and continue to idealise men and desire their approval.' Many of the 150 women she interviewed said they were 'incredibly lucky' to have found their 'perfect' husband. *Our Treacherous Hearts: Why Women Let Men Get Their Way* (1992).

Will the gender struggle outlast the class struggle?

6 | Sociology as a male-dominated discipline

- In the view of Pamela Abbot and Claire Wallace sociology is a 'male dominated discipline' which has 'marginalised feminist knowledge'. Conventional sociology is 'malestream sociology' and fails to give sufficient recognition to the fact that men, the 'first sex', continue to dominate the major institutions of power, *An Introduction To Sociology: Feminist perspectives* (1997).

Only a minority of sociologists mentioned in this book are female – but a majority of 'A' level Sociology students are female!

7 | Checklist of key terms and concepts

Sex and Gender   Biogrammar   Instrumental roles   Expressive roles   Double-shift   Patriarchy   Primary sector of the dual labour market   Secondary sector of the dual labour market   Horizontal segregation   Vertical segregation   Biological reductionism   Masculinism   Genderquake.

8 | Further reading

Abbott, P. and Wallace, C. (1997) *An Introduction to Sociology: Feminist Perspectives* (2nd edition), London, Routledge.

Garrett, S. (1987) *Gender*, London, Tavistock.

Mayes, P. (1986) *Gender*, London, Longman.

Walby, S. (1990) *Theorising Patriarchy*, Blackwell, Oxford.

Chapter nine

Ethnicity and race relations

1 Definitions

Distinguish between prejudice and discrimination.

- **Race:** a social classification based on physical characteristics.

- **Ethnicity:** a shared cultural identity.

- **Prejudice:** hostile and unfavourable attitudes towards members of a particular group.

- **Stereotype:** a rigid and over-simplified belief.

- **Discrimination:** the unequal or differential treatment of people. (Prejudice is attitudinal: a state of mind. Discrimination is behavioural: expressed in actions.)

- **Racism:** the belief that particular individuals are biologically inferior or superior to others.

The old racism was biological. The new racism is cultural.

- **New racism:** hostility towards members of ethnic groups is justified in cultural rather than biological terms. 'A racism which has taken a necessary distance from crude ideas of biological inferiority and superiority now seeks to present an imaginary definition of the nation as a unified cultural community. It constructs and defends an image of national culture – homogeneous in its whiteness yet precarious and perpetually vulnerable to attack from enemies within and without', Paul Gilroy, *There Ain't No Black In The Union Jack* (1987).

- **Institutional racism:** racist assumptions are built into the everyday practices and procedures, rules and routines of organisations.

- **Racialisation:** the process of giving social significance to physical characteristics.

- **A race relations situation:** exists when 'a group of people who are physically distinct: 1) hold rigid beliefs about their social superiority to another group (prejudice); 2) regularly behave towards them in a way which denies them equal access to such resources as jobs, houses, transport and social facilities (discrimination); 3) thereby maintain an unequal distribution of power in society (stratification)', R. Ward in P. Worsley *Problems of Modern Society* (1972).

- **Minorities:** groups who are singled out for differential treatment. G. Simpson and J. Yinger describe a number of possible policies which dominant groups may adopt towards a minority group, *Racial and Cultural Minorities* (1965):

  - Assimilation (forced or permitted)
  - Pluralism
  - Legal protection of minorities
  - Population transfer (peaceful or forced)
  - Subjugation
  - Extermination.

- **Multi-culturalism:** 'the belief that ethnic conflicts can be reduced by greater tolerance and understanding of cultural differences', P. Taylor, *Investigating Culture and Identity* (1997).

- **Anti-racism:** exposing the injustices inflicted on ethnic groups by racist practices.

- **Xenophobia:** an irrational fear or hatred of foreigners.

- **Ethnocentrism:** 'the tendency to look at other cultures through the eyes of one's own culture, and thereby misrepresent them', A. Giddens, *Sociology* (1997).

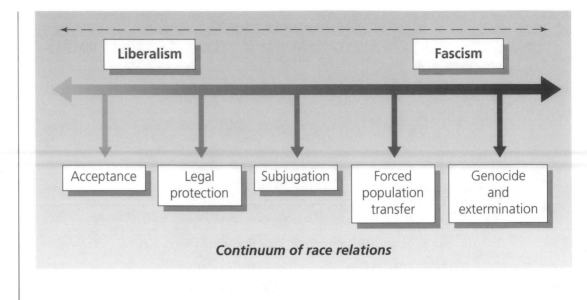

Continuum of race relations

2 | Historical background

- The famines of 1822 and 1846/7 led to mass migration from Ireland. Other immigrant groups which arrived in Britain included Flemish weavers, Huguenot silk manufacturers, Dutch bankers and dyke builders.

- Pogroms in Russia and Poland led to Jewish immigration from 1875 until the passing of the Aliens Act of 1905 – the first law designed to control immigration. The inter-war years were a period of low immigration.

- Black people have lived in Britain since Roman times. From the mid-16th century slaves were brought back from the colonies to work as domestics in fashionable households. At the end of the 18th century black people constituted some 2% of the London population. Post-war immigration from the West Indies dates from June 1948.

- Britain was one of the leading slave-trading nations. From the 16th to the 19th centuries between 10 and 20 million slaves were transported from the west coast of Africa to work on plantations in the Southern USA and the Caribbean.

- Former colonies of the British Empire provided a source of cheap labour for the 'mother country', and organisations like London Transport and the British Hotels and Restaurants Association launched recruitment programmes in the West Indies in the early 1950s.

- Immigration into Britain has been the result of both 'push' factors (low-wages and unemployment in areas like the Caribbean, India, Pakistan, and Bangladesh) and 'pull' factors (job opportunities and higher living standards in Britain).

- Ronald Segal notes that 'From 1871 to 1931 a net outflow of well over 3 million fertilised the rest of the world, especially the Empire, with foreigners from Britain; but that did not make foreigners arriving to fertilise Britain herself any more welcome', *The Race War* (1967).

- In 1995 ethnic minorities represented 5.8% of the population of Britain. 'There are now some 2.6 million non-whites living in the United Kingdom compared with perhaps 100,000 before 1950' – N. Abercrombie *et al.*, *Contemporary British Society* (1994).

- Race riots took place in Cardiff and Liverpool in 1919, and in Notting Hill and Nottingham in 1958. Such racial violence is not new – in 1290 all the Jewish people living in England (some 16,500) were expelled.

- Both Conservative and Labour Governments have introduced laws to limit immigration.

- In 1965 and 1968 racial discrimination and incitement of racial hatred were declared illegal.

Britain has always had a diverse ethnic population.

Distinguish between 'push' factors and 'pull' factors.

3 | Racial disadvantage

'White' and 'black' are problematic terms.

- 'Racial dualism' – the simplistic division of the population into 'white' and 'black' – ignores the increase in the numbers of mixed marriages, and the significant differences which exist between minority groups. 83% of Indian households are owner-occupiers compared with 40% of black households and 36% of Bangladeshi households. A higher proportion of men of Indian origin have professional and managerial jobs than men in the white population. Some 30% of black people aged under 35 have degree qualifications. However, the experience of racism continues to inflict real social disadvantages and injustices on individuals from ethnic minority groups as shown below.

- Brown claims that at least one-third of private employers discriminate against Afro-Caribbean and Asian applicants, in P. Braham (ed.) *Discrimination and Disadvantage in Employment: The Experience of Black Workers* (1981).

- Research with a hidden camera in Bristol for a TV series in 1988 revealed discrimination by landlords of private sector housing. Estate agents, building societies, and council housing departments have been found to practise 'institutional racism'.

- Unemployment rates for young people from minority ethnic groups are nearly twice the rates for young white people. In 1997 the unemployment rate for white men was 9% compared with 27% for Pakistani men.

- Reports by the Home Office and the Commission for Racial Equality have found that Asians and Afro-Caribbeans are far more likely than whites to experience racially motivated attacks. Members of ethnic minorities are more likely to be victims of crime. However, this is also a result of class position and having a younger age structure than the white population, *Sociology Update 1997*.

- In surveys of attitudes more than one-third of respondents described themselves as racially prejudiced – N. Abercrombie *et al.*, *Contemporary British Society* (1994).

- The 1989 Gifford Report reported 'a wholly unacceptable level of racist language and racist behaviour by officers, including officers of rank, in the Merseyside force.' Negative perceptions of the police are more widespread in the black than the white population. In 1991 the Institute of Race Relations recommended that a Royal Commission be set up to investigate deaths in police custody.

Over represented in prison but under-represented in the judiciary.

- According to the Prison Reform Trust the black imprisonment rate in England and Wales is more than seven times higher than for the population as a whole. 'They receive longer prison sentences and are more likely to have probation recommendations ignored' – Andy Barnard and Terry Burgess, *Sociology Examined* (1996).

- In the 1997 General Election only 9 black or South Asian MPs were elected out of a total of 659. 1.47% of senior civil servants are Afro-Caribbean or South Asian. In the armed forces – out of a total of 32,474 officers – 315 officers come from ethnic minorities. Of the 194 Chief Police Officers in England and Wales there is one South Asian. There are no High Court judges from ethnic minority backgrounds. Of the 556 Circuit judges all but four are white, *Sociology Update 1998*.

4 | Theories of ethnic conflict

4.1 Functionalist

- Cultural differences best explain ethnic conflict. All societies are based on a consensus of norms and values. If the culture of a minority group differs significantly from that of the majority, social tensions will arise. However, a process of mutual adaptation can lead to conflict resolution.

- A classic study of cultural factors was *Dark Strangers* (1963) by Sheila Patterson, based on research in Brixton between 1955 and 1958. In late 1950s Britain antipathy to outsiders (xenophobia) was the norm. Until 1939 few inhabitants of Britain had ever met a black person. The race relations situation in Britain was quite different from that of the Southern USA or South Africa where a colour bar had existed for generations. The dynamics of inter-ethnic conflict were explained in terms of an 'immigrant-host' framework. As a result of **acculturation** the newcomers come to share the cultural values of the 'host' community. The 'host' community in turn accommodates itself to the newcomers and **assimilation** (the process of becoming similar) takes place.

- In the functionalist view, ethnic conflict is not inevitable. As cultural differences fade so antagonism between majority and minority groups diminishes.

4.2 Marxist

- Class divisions best explain ethnic conflict, with ethnic minorities constituting the most exploited segment of the working class.

- The relationship between social class and racism was explored by Stephen Castles and Godula Kosack, *Immigrant Workers and Class Structure in Western Europe* (1973). Immigrants (around 5% of the population) were found mainly in the most industrialised countries of Western Europe. Immigration fragmented the working class, because immigrants from poor countries were willing to accept lower wages and this undercut the established workers. 'Immigration helps to give large sections of the indigenous working class the consciousness of a "labour aristocracy" which supports or acquiesces in the exploitation of another section of the working class.'

- The prevalence of white working-class racism is a legacy of colonialism. For centuries the ideology of racial superiority was used to justify territorial conquest, the slave trade, and the exploitation of the economic resources of subject peoples.

- Racism has been 'functional' for the capitalist system's operation by: (1) providing an ideological legitimisation for colonial rule, (2) assisting in the establishment of a 'reserve army' of labour, and (3) fostering divisions within the working class which consolidated the ascendancy of capital.

4.3 Weberian

- Divisions of status and community best explain ethnic conflict and 'ethnicity and communal conflict should be taken as seriously as class and class conflict.' As for the Marxist claim that social class provides a more powerful basis for collective identity than ethnicity Frank Parkin writes: 'Clearly, the inhabitants of Harlem and the Bogside have not been informed of this.' *Marxism and Class Theory. A Bourgeois Critique* (1979).

- A classic Weberian study was *Race, Community and Conflict* (1967) by John Rex and Robert Moore about the Sparkbrook district of Birmingham. A five-year qualification period before individuals could get on to the council housing list meant the cheapest way for immigrants to house themselves was to band together to buy houses in the city's twilight zones and run them as lodging-houses. The existence of distinct 'housing classes' (e.g. outright owners, owner-occupiers, council tenants, and lodging-house tenants) contributed to ethnic conflict. 'Max Weber saw that class struggle was apt to emerge wherever people in a market situation enjoyed differential access to property.'

- At the turn of the century in South Africa a political slogan of the white working class was: 'Workers of the World – Unite For A White South Africa!' Status is distinct from class: individuals who share a common economic position and belong to the same class may still be in ethnic conflict.

5 | Are contemporary social and cultural changes reducing ethnic tensions and conflicts?

Globalisation is a key sociological concept.

- **Yes:** globalisation – the shrinking of time and space by technology and communications – makes ethnic conflict increasingly irrelevant. Barriers between ethnic groups are breaking down, and national cultural identities are becoming more diverse. Paul Gilroy, *The Black Atlantic* (1993) – shows how the black cultures of the Caribbean, the USA and Britain have interacted with each other and developed new hybrid forms and styles. In post-modern and post-traditional societies the fixed boundaries on which ethnic conflict thrives are being eroded.

- **No:** globalisation and the weakening of boundaries between nation states will intensify ethnic conflict. Globalisation is not a one-way movement towards cultural homogeneity. It also generates 'a search to recover lost local traditions, and an emphasis on local cultural identity'. The war in Bosnia could be 'the shape of things to come' rather than 'a residue of the past', A. Giddens: *Beyond Left and Right. The Future of Radical Politics* (1994). Destabilising social change has been accompanied by a resurgence in fundamentalist politics. The disruption of long-established traditions may make individuals more, not less, likely to project their fears of 'The Other' on to members of 'out-groups'.

6 | Checklist of key terms and concepts

- Ethnicity   Prejudice   Discrimination   Stereotype   Ethnocentrism
Racism and New Racism   'Push' factors and 'Pull' factors   Racial dualism
Xenophobia   Acculturation   Assimilation   Globalisation

7 | Further reading

O'Donnell, M. (1991) *Race and Ethnicity*, London, Longman.

Gilroy, P. (1993) *Small Acts. Thoughts on the politics of black cultures*, London, Serpent's Tail.

Mason, D. (1995) *Race and Ethnicity in Modern Britain*, Oxford, Oxford University Press.

Skellington, R. (1996) *'Race' In Britain Today*, London, Sage/Open University Press.

Chapter ten

Crime and deviance

1 Definitions

- **Crime:** behaviour which breaks the law.

- **Criminology:** studies 'the processes of making laws, or breaking laws, and of reacting towards the breaking of laws', Edwin Sutherland, *Principles of Criminology* (1960).

- **Deviance:** behaviour which deviates (departs from) the norms and expectations of a particular society or group.

Most deviance is not criminal.

- **White-collar crime:** illegal actions (such as fraud, tax evasion, insider-dealing, espionage on other companies) committed by high-status individuals in the course of their occupations.

- **Corporate crime:** illegal actions which are knowingly committed by executives who control business corporations (e.g. actions which cause damage to the public such as poisoning the environment).

- **Crimes of the powerful:** illegal actions committed by individuals who hold positions of status and authority (such as members of governments or top civil servants).

- **Criminal and deviant behaviour:** violates both legal and social rules (e.g. a son assaulting his mother).

- **Criminal but not deviant behaviour:** violates legal rules but may not be perceived as violating social rules (e.g. dropping litter, small-scale tax evasion, driving just above the speed limit).

- **Deviant but not criminal behaviour:** violates social rules but not legal rules (e.g. eating with one's hands rather than a knife and fork, snoring during a play).

It is not what you do – it is where and when you do it!

- **Time, place and context:** determine whether an action is defined as criminal or deviant (e.g. **time:** washing the car at 3 a.m. rather than 3 p.m.; **place:** standing naked by the front door rather than in the bathroom; **context:** singing in a public library rather than in a public house).

2 Theories of crime

2.1 Biological and genetic

- Early criminologists believed that violent criminals were driven by their distinctive biological make-up. Giambattista della Porta (1536–1615) measured the heads and bodies of violent criminals. Cesare Lombroso (1836–1909), an Italian army doctor, believed that criminals possess special physical features ('high cheek bones... handle-shaped ears...extremely acute sight...'). A violent criminal was someone with the body and mind of our primitive ancestors.

- More recently it has been claimed that individuals become criminals because they possess a 'criminal gene'.

- Critics point out that if crime was caused by a 'criminal gene' individuals could not be held to be responsible for their actions because it was not 'them' but their genes which caused the offence to be committed.

- In *The New Criminology* (1973) Taylor, Walton and Young write that 'Individuals with pronounced physical stigmata may be evaluated differently from those without such physical markings by others in the course of ongoing social interaction. A self-fulfilling prophecy, therefore, in which the individual carries out the other's expectations of him, is entirely possible.'

2.2 Functionalist

If criminals went on strike unemployment would soar!

- Deviance is seen as a normal and inevitable aspect of social life. Durkheim believed that even in a society of saints some saints would conform to norms more closely than others and the 'deviant' saints would have to be punished. Punishing deviants is 'functional' – it helps to clarify the norms of behaviour and strengthen the moral consensus.

- Crime keeps large numbers of people in employment and generates economic activity (e.g. probation officers, judges, lawyers, prison officers, police officers, security guards, manufacturers of security devices, locksmiths, criminology lecturers, etc.).

- In *Social Theory and Social Structure* (1949) Robert Merton used the concept of anomie (the breakdown in the norms which regulate behaviour) to develop a functionalist theory of crime. Every society promotes certain cultural goals and lays down the normative means by which these goals are to be achieved. In the USA the majority of people accept both the goals and the means (they are **conformists**). But large numbers break the law in order to acquire money (**innovators**). Some individuals (like tramps and drop-outs) give up on both goals and means (**retreatists**). Others just go through the motions but no longer believe they will ever become rich (**ritualists**). A minority put forward a new set of goals and means (**rebels**).

- Critics dispute Merton's view that all sections of the population share the same cultural goals. Not all crime is motivated by a desire for money (e.g. vandalism). Some cultures have pathologically high levels of destructive crime, and it is difficult to see how this can be 'functional' for the social system.

2.3 Marxist

Inequality + exploitation + alienation = crime.

- Marx and Engels did not develop a systematic theory of crime. In *The Eighteenth Brumaire of Louis Bonaparte* (1852) Marx described how 'crimes of the powerful' were committed by a section of the French military establishment in alliance with the lumpenproletariat (e.g. 'ruined and adventurous offshoots of the bourgeoisie... vagabonds, discharged soldiers, escaped galley slaves, swindlers ... this scum, offal, refuse of all classes...').

- Crime is a manifestation of an unjust social order. The primary purpose of the 'repressive state apparatus' (police, courts, prisons, etc.) is to protect the private interests of the wealthy rather than to safeguard the public interest. The legal system is biased in favour of those who are wealthy enough to hire the best lawyers.

- Working-class crime (such as petty theft) is a response to social disadvantage. If governments were really serious about reducing crime they would take steps to deal with the unequal distribution of wealth and income.

- Class bias is evident in the social composition of the judiciary (80% of judges attended private schools); in the operation of magistrates' courts (working-class defendants are unfamiliar with the 'rules of the game'); and in the state's responses to different types of crime (e.g. to social security fraud compared with tax evasion – or 'tax planning' as corporate accountants describe it).

- Some organised crime (e.g. drug-trafficking) takes place with the active collusion of police, government officials and 'reputable' financial institutions. The law is far more rigorously enforced on street corners than in board rooms. Illegal action committed by trade unions is seen as much more serious than illegal action committed by trans-national corporations.

- New Right theorists celebrate the virtues of capitalism, but fail to see the possibility that capitalist values may generate crime. This has been described as the 'Tantalos syndrome': capitalist societies tantalise individuals with images of consumer goods which they cannot afford to buy. Crime is the inevitable result.

- Critics argue that many crimes (e.g. child abuse and rape) cannot be explained in terms of economic inequality. Crime is often a product of selfish and aggressive values, and some marxists seem to believe that the working class has been miraculously 'immunised' from such values.

2.4 Left Realism

- An approach developed by neo-Marxists who accepted the Marxist view that inequalities in the distribution of wealth and life-chances cause much crime, but criticised Marxism for being too economically deterministic. It dismissed as romantic idealism the view of the working-class criminal as a kind of 'Robin Hood' figure heroically engaged in redistributing resources from rich to poor.

- Most working-class crime is **intra-class** rather than **inter-class** (i.e. the majority of its victims are working class). The high crime rate is a real social problem and not an alarmist myth dreamt up by right-wing ideologues.

- Left Realism has its origins in the 'New Criminology' which combined structuralist and social action approaches and saw crime as the product of both conscious choice and specific social circumstances.

- Jock Young (the leading Left Realist theorist) argues that a combination of policies is needed to tackle the crime problem. Inequality and unemployment must be reduced, the social cohesion of communities strengthened, crime made more difficult to carry out, and more effective detection and sentencing introduced to deter people from committing crime.

- Critics argue that Left Realism has succumbed to a 'moral panic' on crime. Some of its policy proposals are naïve (e.g. calls for wealth and income redistribution will be ignored by government). Other policy proposals could result in more heavy-handed policing of inner city areas and more people being sent to prison.

2.5 Labelling and interactionist theory

- In *Outsiders. Studies in the Sociology of Deviance* (1963) Howard Becker argued that 'deviant behaviour is behaviour that people so label'. It is not what you do but its social context which determines whether your actions are labelled as deviant or not. (In peacetime individuals who kill other people are labelled as deviant; in wartime individuals who refuse to kill other people are labelled as deviant.)

- The social control system can change individuals' identities from 'normal' to 'deviant' and set them on course for a **deviant career**. The **stigma** of a criminal record changes a person's self-image. Appearing in court and being publicly sentenced is a form of status degradation. **Primary deviants** (who see themselves as basically law-abiding even though they occasionally commit minor offences) are transformed into **secondary deviants** (who see themselves as criminals and deliberately follow a life of crime).

- Studies of prisons have found that some 70% have been 'inside' before. The majority of inmates are **recidivists** (individuals who habitually relapse into crime). The label of 'criminal' functions as a **master status** and over-shadows all other aspects of a person's identity. A **self-fulfilling prophecy** results in individuals coming to see themselves as others see them.

- Critics reject the view that individuals are made into secondary deviants by the labels police and courts 'stick' on them. Labelling theorists ignore the possibility that individuals may actually decide to become criminals. The label follows the crime rather than vice versa.

Social disadvantage + individual choice = crime.

'Give a dog a bad name. . . .'

Self-fulfilling prophecy is a key sociological concept.

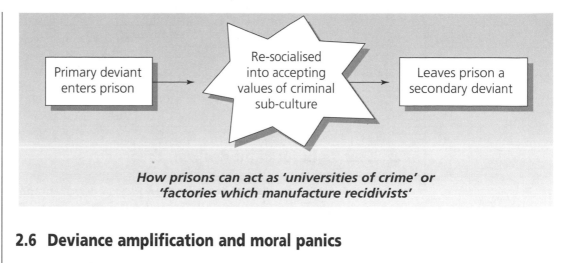

How prisons can act as 'universities of crime' or 'factories which manufacture recidivists'

2.6 Deviance amplification and moral panics

- A group is labelled as 'deviant' by the mass media, social concern grows, and an increase (amplification) in deviant and criminal behaviour occurs. The classic study of this is *Folk Devils and Moral Panics: the Creation of the Mods and Rockers* (1980) by Stanley Cohen. 'Societies appear to be subject every now and then to periods of moral panic. A condition, episode, person or group of persons emerges to become defined as a threat to societal values and interests. . . the moral barricades are manned by editors, bishops, politicians and other right-thinking people...'

- In 1964 the 'Folk Devils' were mods and rockers who (so newspapers alleged) sought to disrupt the peace and tranquillity of the Easter week-end at Clacton. The police and the courts were urged to 'crack down hard' on this new social problem. On the following Bank Holiday more mods and rockers arrived at seaside resorts, more police were mobilised to confront them, more arrests were made, more mods and rockers arrived....

- Critics point out that just because newspapers start a 'moral panic' does not necessarily mean there is nothing to panic about. 'Panic' can signify legitimate public concern (e.g. the campaign to ban handguns following the killing of 16 children in Dunblane in 1996). Also, moral panics do not always lead to an amplification of deviance (e.g. the prison sentences given to those in the 1958 Notting Hill race riots were followed by a de-amplification in deviance).

Think of other examples of 'moral panics'.

2.7 Sub-cultural theories

- The 1920s Chicago Ecological School found that inner city and working-class areas had significantly higher rates of recorded crime than middle-class and suburban areas.

- Crime is 'almost a social tradition' in some districts in Britain, J.B. Mays; *Growing Up In The City* (1954). Criminal sub-cultures are most likely to flourish in areas of acute social disadvantage, James Patrick, *A Glasgow Gang Observed* (1973). R. Cloward and L.E. Ohlin found that delinquent groups are most common in socially disadvantaged areas where the chances of gaining wealth legitimately are small, *Delinquency and Opportunity* (1960).

- According to **differential association theory** the likelihood of engaging in crime is determined by the values and attitudes of the people one associates with. Someone who grows up mixing with law-breakers and who sees crime as a common occurrence will view crime as acceptable.

- Albert Cohen's *Delinquent Boys* (1955) found that **status deprivation** was a key factor in joining a delinquent group. A status-deprived 'failure' at school becomes a 'king' in the streets. A study of young thieves in London found that they stole so as to be 'accepted as one of the group, to gain prestige', William Belson, *Juvenile Theft* (1975).

- Critics see sub-cultural theory as too deterministic – it ignores the role of individual choice. Not everyone who grows up in an area with a high crime-rate becomes a criminal. In *Delinquency and Drift* (1964) David Matza argues that individuals use

Status deprivation is a key sociological concept.

techniques of neutralisation to explain their deviant behaviour away (e.g. 'I drank too much'). *Subterranean values* of pleasure-seeking and risk-taking are found in mainstream suburban society as well as in 'problem' areas. Everyone is deviant at some time or other, and young people are particularly prone to drifting into crime by chance. Neo-Marxist theory sees some sub-cultures as representing a conscious challenge to the stabilised order.

2.8 New Right (or Right Realism) theory

- This rejects the view that crime is linked to social disadvantage as over the last four decades both living standards and crime have risen dramatically. Crime rates were much lower in the economically depressed years of the 1930s.

- Individuals are rational, autonomous agents responsible for their own actions. 'Tender' minded approaches which assumed that criminals could be re-educated and rehabilitated were tried in the 1960s – and failed.

- The state should give out clear signals about moral boundaries and the costs individuals face if they engage in crime. In the USA 'three strikes and you are out!' policies are used (i.e. three convictions automatically means 25 years' imprisonment).

- *New administrative criminology (NAC)* advocates 'target hardening' measures to make it more difficult to commit crime. Much crime is opportunist, petty rather than serious. The development of closed-circuit television (CCTV) demonstrates how technological innovation can improve detection and clear-up rates. Individuals are generally selfish and have to be kept in line by effective surveillance systems and deterrence.

- The increase in crime is a symptom of a wider cultural malaise. There has been a decline in 'civility', in respect for authority, in the work ethic, and – owing to increased welfare dependency – in family life. To reduce crime these broader social and cultural issues will also have to be addressed.

- Critics point out that despite very high imprisonment rates in the USA and (in many states) the death penalty, the rates of violent crime are amongst the highest in the industrial world. Home Office projections anticipate that the numbers in British prisons will reach 74,500 by the year 2005. (So much for the theory that sending more people to prison will act as a deterrent.) A relationship clearly exists between crime and deprivation – otherwise crime rates would not be highest in socially disadvantaged areas. Even in the pre-consumer society of the 1930s economic depression was followed by an increase in the crime rate.

2.9 Theory caveat (warning)

- Anthony Giddens points out: 'even though "crime" is only one subcategory of deviant behaviour as a whole, it covers such a variety of forms of activity – from taking a bar of chocolate without paying, to mass murder – that it is unlikely that we could produce a single theory which would account for all forms of criminal conduct', *Sociology* (1997).

3 | Women and crime

- In recent years the female crime rate has increased more rapidly than the male – even though females are far less likely to be convicted of crime than males. There are some 24 times more male prisoners than female prisoners. Only in offences relating to prostitution are more females convicted than males (although in shoplifting women are not far behind). Women appear in crime statistics mainly as victims. Crime is predominantly a male activity.

Most crime is male crime!

3.1 Explanations for the lower female crime rate

1 **differential socialisation:** 'femininity' has been associated with domesticity and caring, 'masculinity' with toughness and risk-taking.

2 **social control:** because females have traditionally spent more time at home their lives have been more tightly regulated and controlled than males.

3 **peer group pressure:** pressure towards conformist behaviour is greater amongst females than males, e.g. girls who have numerous sexual partners risk being denigrated as deviant – as 'slags' – while there is no male equivalent to this term.

4 **opportunity:** crime rates peak during adolescence, a time when males spend less time in the home than females. In the past limited female employment meant females had fewer chances to commit crime in the workplace. The great majority of white-collar crime, corporate crime, and organised crime is committed by males. However, the female crime rate is increasing with more females in paid employment.

3.2 Female fear of crime

> The British Crime Survey is a key research study.

- Many crimes of violence and sexual assault inflicted on women in their homes are never reported to the police. Women are more likely to be assaulted by their male partners than by strangers. On average, every three days a woman in Britain dies of domestic violence.

- The British Crime Survey dating from 1982 has found that a much higher proportion of women (especially older ones) feel 'very unsafe' in the street after dark than men, even though women are three times less likely to be attacked by a stranger than men.

- *Attitudes to Punishment* (1997) by M. Hough and J. Roberts found that the British public overestimate the extent of crime. 75% believe crime is on the increase, but in 1993–97 there was an 8% fall in crime reported to the police. Most people believe that more than a third of all crimes involve sex and violence, but the official figure is around 6%.

3.3 The validity of female crime statistics

> Are females more successful at hiding their crime?

- Official crime statistics may understate the number of crimes by women. A **chivalry factor** could operate with police and judges being more lenient towards females. Females are more likely than males to be given a conditional discharge, and to be cautioned rather than prosecuted. They receive shorter prison sentences than males. However, research has found that females who deviate from gender-role expectations and who do not behave in court in a stereotypical helpless, tearful and 'feminine' way risk being punished more severely than males.

- **Self-report studies** (where individuals list, in confidence, crimes they have committed) have found that the gap in the male–female crime rate is not as wide as the official statistics suggest. Nonetheless females still 'self-report' fewer crimes than males, and they are less likely to 'self-report' serious crimes (such as those involving violence).

4 Ethnicity and crime

- Afro-Caribbeans are seven times more likely to be in prison as the white or Asian population. In the 1960s the crime rate for the first generation of Afro-Caribbean immigrants was much lower than that for the general population. Between 1972 and 1976 'the definition of blacks as a low crime group turned around 180 degrees', Paul Gilroy *There Ain't no Black in the Union Jack* (1987). The Brixton disorders in 1981 signalled a crisis in relations between the Metropolitan Police and the Afro-Caribbean community.

4.1 Explanations for ethnic crime rate differentials

- **Racist labelling.** Lord Scarman's *Report* (1981) into the Brixton disorders acknowledged that 'racial prejudice does manifest itself occasionally in the behaviour of a few officers in the streets.' According to Paul Gilroy: 1. Britain's history as a colonial power has created a legacy of racist attitudes and 'racist ideologies of black crime and criminality' have been widely propagated. 2. the police deliberately exaggerated the extent of crime in the black community. 3. some of the crime committed by black youth can be seen as a form of anti-colonial political struggle, *The Empire Strikes Back. Race and Racism in 70s Britain* (1982). In the 1980s 'Stop and Search' operations targeted black youths in inner city areas. A report by the Policy Research Institute (1984) concluded that racist attitudes were widespread amongst the lower ranks of the Metropolitan Police.

- **Social exclusion and disadvantage.** Left Realists like Jock Young and John Lea argue that high rates of street crime are the result of poverty, unemployment, discrimination, denial of equal opportunities, and social marginalisation. Young Afro-Caribbean males tend to live in areas of multiple deprivation where employment opportunities are limited. Racist labelling has inflated the official statistics of street crime. However, Young and Lea claim that in the early 1980s 'there was a real rise in crime among the West Indian population, and the police, in responding to it, were not responding simply to figments of their imagination.' *What Is To Be Done About Law And Order?* (1984).

5 | Official crime statistics

- In England and Wales records of 'crimes made known to the police' (CKP) have been kept since 1857.

- The official crime rate remained relatively constant until the 1930s, rose gradually until the mid-1950s, and more dramatically in the 1960s and 1970s. During the 1980s recorded crime doubled.

- In 1997 in England and Wales 4.6 million notifiable offences were recorded by the police. This fall of nearly 9% on 1996 was the largest drop in post-war history. However, violent crime rose by 1.7%.

5.1 Limitations of official crime statistics

- **Some crimes are not reported to the police:** they may be seen as too trivial to report; victims may feel embarrassed (e.g. in cases of sexual offences or violence in the home); they may be unaware that they are victims of a crime (e.g. in cases of fraud or where there are poor accounting facilities in a store); there may be a lack of confidence in the police's ability to solve the crime; victims may fear reprisals from criminals or may decide to take action against the criminals themselves.

- **Some crimes are much more likely to be reported to the police than others:** cases of petty theft are less likely to be reported than cases of serious assault or stolen cars (where insurance claims will be made).

- **Not all offences reported to the police are recorded as crimes:** the police decide whether or not an offence is serious enough to be classified as a crime. It has been estimated that only around 40% of reported offences are recorded as crimes (with this proportion varying considerably between constabularies).

- **The exercise of police discretion has an influence on crime statistics:** a new Chief Constable appointed in Manchester prioritised tackling pornography, which led to a dramatic increase in the number of recorded crimes for this offence. A change in police strategy from informal community policing to 'strict' policing (or vice versa) will

Racist labelling and/or social disadvantage?

Does a rise in the official crime rate mean a rise in the 'real' crime rate?

change the crime rate. The assumptions police make about who is a 'typical' criminal (e.g. young, male, working class, belonging to a particular ethnic group, etc.) will make it more likely that individuals who fit this stereotype will be prosecuted.

- **Moral panics will affect the crime rate:** a particular group is stereotyped by the mass media, the police and the courts 'stamp down hard', and deviance amplification takes place.

- **Changes in legislation, technology, and police manpower influence crime statistics:** some actions may cease to be defined as crimes (e.g. certain forms of homosexuality and abortion). Non-criminal actions may be redefined as crimes (e.g. not wearing a seat belt). Increased telephone ownership makes it easier for the public to report crimes. More sophisticated technology makes it easier for the police to detect and solve crime. The police-to-population ratio has more than doubled since 1861.

- **Social and economic changes can influence crime statistics:** in a consumer society there are more goods for people to steal. (Research suggests that over a 4-year period for every 1% rise in consumer spending, thefts and burglaries are likely to rise by 2%.) The growth of insurance increases the incentive for people to report property crimes; the decline in close-knit communities makes it more likely that people will report crime to the authorities rather than dealing with it informally; changes in norms and values make it more likely that crimes such as child abuse and domestic violence will be reported.

Examiners expect you to know these two research methods.

- **Victim studies and self-report studies:** in victim studies individuals list the crimes they have experienced over a period of time. In self-report studies individuals list the undetected crimes they have committed over a period of time. Both studies reveal that crime is underestimated by official statistics. The 1996 British Crime Survey found that in 1995 only 41% of crimes were reported to the police. (The term **dark figure** refers to criminal activity not recorded in official statistics.)

6 Football hooliganism

- Between the late 1960s and the mid-1980s football-related violence has received considerable media attention. Although it has declined it continues to be a social problem (e.g. in 1998 a football supporter was killed outside Gillingham football ground). Key studies include:

Class, gender, age and nationalism are key factors in football hooliganism.

- *Hooligan: A History of Respectable Fears* (1983) by Geoffrey Pearson. Football hooliganism is not new. In 1314 the Mayor of London complained about a 'great uproar in the city' which accompanied the 'striking of footballs' and the word 'hooligan' entered the popular vocabulary in 1898.

- *Soccer Consciousness and Soccer Hooliganism* (1971) by Ian Taylor (in *Images of Deviance*, ed. S. Cohen (1971). Football hooliganism is an attempt by the working class to assert control over a game which has become middle class, commercialised, and remote from the local community. In the 1970s sections of the working class resorted to hooliganism to 'assert some inarticulate but keenly experienced sense of control over "the game that was theirs".'

- *Knuckle Sandwich. Growing Up In The Working-Class City* (1978) by David Robins and Philip Cohen. Football supporters attempt to 'magically' rediscover a sense of belonging and community and hooliganism erupts when the home 'turf' is threatened by rival supporters.

- *Football and working-class fans: tradition and change* (1978) (in 'Football Hooliganism: the Wider Context', ed. R. Ingham). This relates the growth of football hooliganism in the 1970s to increased affluence, the rise of youth culture, and the decline in social control of the young by the older generation.

- *Rules of Disorder* (1978) by Peter Marsh, Elizabeth Rosser and Rom Harré. More people have died in (fire-prone) theatres than in football grounds. 'Symbolic aggression' (chanting and name-calling) rather than 'real' aggression is the norm at the vast majority of matches.

- *Hooligans Abroad. The Behaviour and Control of English Fans in Continental Europe* (1984) by John Williams, Eric Dunning and Patrick Murphy. Football hooliganism is closely linked to an aggressive masculine style prevalent in the lower working class. 'Modes of behaviour are engaged in that are more openly violent than the dominant norms demand.'

- *The Roots of Football Hooliganism: An Historical and Sociological Study* (1988) by Dunning, Murphy and Williams. Football hooliganism comes from a number of inter-related factors: aggressive masculinity, the growing divide between the 'rougher' and more 'respectable' sections of the working class, the virtual collapse of the youth labour market, racism, nationalism, and changes in the mass media.

- *Post-Fandom and the Millennial Blues* (1997) by Steve Redhead. The male 'terrace' soccer culture of 'fandom' has now come to an end. The 'fan' has been replaced by the 'post-fan' who 'does not have to leave the home or the bar … because television and video provide endless opportunity for "grazing" and "channel surfing". Football hooliganism ceased to be fashionable in the mid-1980s. Redhead's post-modernist conclusion is that 'there is no such thing as "real" soccer hooliganism'.

Was football hooliganism a 1980s cultural fashion?

7 | Suicide

- Suicide is a form of deviance which was defined as a crime until 1961.

- The classic work *Suicide. A Study In Sociology* (1897) was written by Emile Durkheim whose aims included establishing the credibility of sociology as a scientific discipline and exposing the inadequacy of 19th-century views of the causes of suicide (e.g. that it was the result of innate biological factors or climatic conditions). Suicide was defined as 'deliberate and intended death'.

- Industrialisation in France was accompanied by a sharp rise in the official suicide rate. Durkheim sought to show that suicide, though a most personal act, was shaped by broader social forces.

- Durkheim was the first sociologist to carry out systematic analysis of official statistics. This revealed that the suicide rate was determined by the degree of social integration and social solidarity in society, by the vitality of group life.

- Durkheim classified suicide into four types:

  1 **egoistic suicide:** individuals are insufficiently integrated into a group

  2 **altruistic suicide:** individuals are so strongly integrated into a group that they sacrifice their lives for it

  3 **anomic suicide:** there is a breakdown in the stable norms and values which regulate individuals' lives

  4 **fatalistic suicide:** individuals experience excessive regulation and discipline (e.g. prisoners and slaves).

- Durkheim concluded that 'suicide varies inversely with the degree of integration of the social groups of which the individual forms a part.', i.e. the stronger the group ties in a society, the lower the suicide rate. The suicide rate is determined by the social structure.

Durkheim is the classic theorist of suicide. You will need to be able to explain and evaluate his theory.

7.1 Did Durkheim's theory make a real contribution to our understanding of suicide?

Yes:

- Official statistics on suicide support Durkheim's analysis. He described the family as a 'powerful safeguard against suicide.' Individuals who have close family ties (e.g. those

A key Durkheimian theme is the degree of group integration in society.

married with children) have lower suicide rates than individuals without such ties (e.g. the single or divorced).

- Those who live in close-knit communities have lower suicide rates than those living in the anonymous bed-sit districts of large cities. 'Solitary' occupations have higher suicide rates than 'sociable' occupations (e.g. more psychiatrists commit suicide than physiotherapists). War strengthens group integration and this leads to a fall in the suicide rate.

- Individuals who become unemployed or bankrupt are more likely to commit suicide (anomie).

- In the view of Anthony Giddens 'social factors have a fundamental influence on suicidal behaviour... (Durkheim's study) remains a classic work whose relevance to sociology is by no means exhausted today', *Sociology* (1997).

No:

- The positivist assumptions on which Durkheim's theory was based were fundamentally flawed. Official statistics on suicide are social constructions which lack 'objective' validity. Coroners reach suicide verdicts on the basis of 'common-sense' assumptions. Only if an individual conforms to the stereotyped image of a 'typical' suicide (e.g. ill and depressed) is a suicide verdict given. Only a minority of those who commit suicide leave suicide notes.

- Many deaths which are classified as road accidents may well be suicides. Suicide verdicts may not be given in order to spare families further grief.

- In Catholic countries (where suicide is regarded as a sin) official statistics will significantly understate the number of suicides.

- It is impossible to establish the 'real' suicide rate. Some individuals deliberately gamble with fate and are unsure of whether they intend to live or die. Some 20 serious suicide attempts (parasuicide) are made for every suicide.

- Durkheim's theory neglected the role of individual psychological factors. Jean Baechler (a contemporary of Durkheim) argued that every suicide has a unique meaning. Suicide may be 'escapist' (flight from an intolerable situation, grief, or an act of atonement for an imagined fault); or 'aggressive' (an act of vengeance to provoke remorse). Durkheim ignores these complexities.

Interactionists are critical of Durkheim's positivist approach.

8 | Checklist of key terms and concepts

White-collar crime   Corporate crime   Crimes of the powerful   Deviant career
Conformists, Innovators, Retreatists, Ritualists, and Rebels Intra-class and Inter-class
crime Stigma   Primary deviant and Secondary deviant   Recidivist   Master status
Self-fulfilling prophecy   Differential Association Theory   Status deprivation
Moral panic   Subterranean values   Techniques of neutralisation   Tantalos syndrome
CKP   Chivalry factor   Victim studies   Self-report studies   Dark figure   Parasuicide
Egoistic, Anomic, Altruistic, and Fatalistic suicide

9 | Further Reading

Aggleton, P. (1991), *Deviance*, London, Routledge.

Lea, J. and Young, J. (1993) *What is to be Done about Law and Order? Crisis in the Nineties*, London, Pluto Press.

Moore, S. (1996) *Investigating Deviance*, 2nd edition, London, Collins Educational.

Walklate, S. (1995) *Gender and Crime*, Hemel Hempstead, Prentice Hall / Harvester Wheatsheaf.

Chapter eleven

Education

1 | Definition

- Education is the 'process of acquiring knowledge and skills, both formally and informally', *The Complete A – Z Sociology Handbook* by T. Lawson and J. Garrod (1996).

- Informal education takes place within the family and community. Formal education – schooling or systematic learning – takes place in specialist institutions.

- Emile Durkheim defined education as 'the methodical socialisation of the young generation.'

2 | Development of the educational system

- A Royal Commission in 1858 under the Duke of Newcastle concluded that a compulsory national educational system was 'neither attainable or desirable.' Britain was an educationally underdeveloped society: in 1840 a third of men, and a half of women, could not write.

- The 1870 Elementary Education Act laid the foundations for free compulsory education. In 1880 schooling was made compulsory up to the age of 10, and in 1918 elementary education was made free.

- Recruitment for the Boer War (1899–1902) highlighted educational and physical deficiencies in the population. The 1902 Education Act created the administrative framework for a national system of secondary education and established the local education authority (LEA).

- The Free Place Regulations of 1907 made government grants to secondary schools conditional on providing 25% of free places to pupils from elementary schools. Secondary education was opened up to the working class.

- The 1918 Education Act abolished elementary school fees and raised the school leaving age to 14. (It was raised to 15 in 1947, and 16 in 1973.)

- The 1944 Education Act provided free secondary education and introduced the selective tripartite system. Children were divided into three intellectual groups: grammar school (high intelligence); technical school (higher grade practical); and secondary modern (lower grade practical).

- 1965: the Labour Government's Circular 10/65 instructed local authorities to reorganise secondary education on comprehensive lines.

- The 1980 Education Act introduced the assisted places scheme. Children from less well-off families who gained places at private schools had all or some of their fees paid for by the state. Parents were able to express a preference about their child's school. (The assisted places scheme was abolished in 1998.)

- The 1988 Education Reform Act set up a national curriculum of core and foundation subjects for all state schools. Attainment testing was introduced. Schools could 'opt-out' of local authority control and acquire grant-maintained status under which they were funded by central government. Local School Management (LSM) enabled schools to manage their own funds. More day-to-day decision making was devolved to school governors (some of whom were parent governors).

- The Government believed the **marketisation** of education would improve standards by providing a variety of schools for consumers (i.e. pupils and their parents) to choose

Compulsory primary schooling was introduced in 1880.

Examiners will expect you to be familiar with the Tripartite system.

from. The most successful schools would attract the most customers, and would be rewarded with extra funding. Schools with falling rolls would be closed down unless they responded to market competition and improved their performance.

- Critics of marketisation claimed it would deepen social divisions. Children with middle-class parents would gain places at high-status and well-resourced schools. Children from socially disadvantaged families would be concentrated in under-resourced schools at the bottom of the educational hierarchy.

3 | Theoretical perspectives and education

3.1 Functionalism

- According to Emile Durkheim education is 'above all the means by which society perpetually recreates the conditions of its very existence.'

- In pre-industrial society a way of life is passed on to a new generation by family and kin. In industrial society education is separated (differentiated) from other aspects of socialisation.

- Talcott Parsons describes the classroom as a 'mini-society' – 'an agency through which individual personalities are trained to be motivationally and technically adequate to the performance of adult roles.'

- Education performs a role-allocation function: talents are measured and assessed, and individuals allocated to positions in the occupational structure.

- Education performs a social control function. A 1906 Board of Education Report stressed the need for 'habits of discipline and ready obedience', and declared that education should make children 'efficient members of the class to which they will belong.'

- Critics see functionalists as viewing pupils mechanically, as passive recipients of social control rather than as interacting and autonomous individuals. The values transmitted in schools are based on those of the dominant class rather than reflecting a true cultural consensus. The educational system does not provide a meritocratic ladder of opportunity but confirms most individuals in their existing class positions.

3.2 Marxism

- Karl Marx believed 'the class which is the dominant material force in society is at the same time its dominant intellectual force.' Schools form part of what Louis Althusser called the **state ideological apparatus** and seek to inculcate ruling class ideology into the population.

- **Correspondence theorists** such as Samuel Bowles and Herbert Gintis see authority relationships in the classroom as corresponding to those of the workplace. At school, individuals from working-class backgrounds learn to obey, do what they are told, and to accept authority. Individuals who attend public schools are prepared for their future roles by acquiring 'leadership' skills.

- The educational system functions as a mechanism for the reproduction of social inequality. Children attend schools which reflect their parents' class location (e.g. the children of the poor attend 'sink' comprehensive schools). One of the key functions of examinations is to legitimise inequality.

- Critics see Marxists as too rigid and deterministic. Pupils do not passively accept either their teachers' ideological beliefs or their own place in the class structure. Rather than acting as a mechanism for the reproduction of class divisions, the educational system has enabled large numbers of pupils from working-class backgrounds to be upwardly mobile.

3.3 Interpretive approaches (action theory)

- The face-to-face interactions which occur inside the micro world of the school and the classroom significantly influence pupils' success and failure in education.

- A key concept is the **self-fulfilling prophecy**. Teachers' expectations powerfully affect educational achievement. Individuals labelled as 'bright' develop positive self-images and are motivated to work harder. Individuals labelled as 'dim' are de-motivated and pushed into failure. Robert Rosenthal and Leonora Jacobson conducted an experiment in an elementary school in California. 20% of the pupils were selected at random and the teachers told that these pupils would soon make rapid intellectual progress. A year later it was found that the randomly selected 20% had made the highest gains in test scores in intelligence tests. Because their teachers started to believe in them the pupils started to believe in themselves, *Pygmalion in the Classroom* (1968).

- Teachers share a similar picture of the **ideal pupil**. Middle-class pupils fit this ideal most closely, and tend to be placed in top streams and encouraged to study subjects with high academic status. Working-class pupils are generally placed in lower streams and encouraged to study practical and vocational subjects.

- Critics see action theorists as failing to recognise the fact that the economic and cultural capital in a child's home has a powerful influence on educational attainment. Not all pupils accept the labels (whether positive or negative) applied to them by their teachers.

Action theorists focus on micro processes of interaction rather than macro social structures.

Labelling theory is a key theme in research in both education and crime.

4 | Social class and education

- *Education and the Working Class. Some general themes raised by a study of 88 working-class children in a northern industrial city* (1962) by Brian Jackson and Dennis Marsden. Academically successful working-class pupils who went to university were found to come from similar social backgrounds. The number of children in their families was smaller than average; the majority lived in districts where the social classes were mixed; one of the parents (usually the mother) was 'sunken middle class' and had attended a grammar school; a majority of the families were owner-occupiers; most of the fathers were foremen or supervisors; they formed 'a kind of working-class aristocracy.'

- *The Home and the School* (1964) and *All Our Future* (1968) by J.W.B.Douglas. This longitudinal study of 5,362 children born in 1946 found that educational attainment was influenced by: 1. The parents: middle-class parents took more interest in their child's educational progress. 2. Size of family: children from smaller families were most successful at school. 3. Position in family: eldest children were more successful than either younger children or only children. 4. Housing conditions: pupils living in homes rented from private landlords obtained fewer grammar school places than expected from their measured ability. 5. Regional inequalities: the proportion of grammar school places available was much higher in Wales than in the south of England.

- *Down Stream. Failure in the Grammar School* (1965) by R.R. Dale and S. Griffith. This study of a co-educational grammar school found that deterioration in pupils' academic performance was influenced by: 1. Lack of parental encouragement (closely related to the parents' own educational background). 2. Level of parental culture (e.g. general knowledge, vocabulary, access to books). 3. Degree of peer-group support for studying. 4. Poverty: there was an association between early leaving and financial difficulties.

- *Schooling in Capitalist America. Educational Reform and the Contradictions of Economic Life* (1976) by Samuel Bowles and Herbert Gintis. This Marxist analysis shows how the educational system reproduces the class structure. 'Through the educational encounter, individuals are induced to accept the degree of powerlessness

This study is an example of correspondence theory.

with which they will be faced as mature workers.' That working-class parents 'favour stricter educational methods is a reflection of their own work experiences...That professional and self-employed parents prefer a more open atmosphere...is similarly a reflection of their position in the social division of labour.'

- *Learning to Labour. How working-class kids get working-class jobs* (1977) by Paul Willis. Focused on a group of 12 non-academic, working-class lads attending a school near Birmingham. They had no interest in gaining qualifications, and felt superior to their teachers and to conformist pupils. The 'guerrilla warfare of the classroom and corridor' was a sound preparation for the labouring jobs taken on leaving school.

Cultural capital is a key sociological concept.

- *Reproduction. In Education, Society and Culture* (1977) by Pierre Bourdieu and Jean-Claude Passeron. Families pass on a particular *habitus* (forms of taste, behaviour and ways of thinking) to their children. The habitus of middle- and upper-class families includes a high level of cultural capital (i.e. wealth in the form of knowledge, skills with language, familiarity with 'high' culture, etc.). Individuals who do not possess such capital will not climb very far up the educational status ladder.

- *Origins and Destinations* (1980) by A.H. Halsey, A. Heath and J.M. Ridge. The numbers in higher education have increased dramatically since 1944, yet class inequalities continue. Universities are dominated by students from privileged backgrounds. 'Family climate' (a combination of favourable material circumstances and a high level of cultural capital) is the key factor in educational success. Cultural capital has an important influence on choice of secondary school, but material factors become increasingly significant from the age of eleven on (e.g. low-income families find it difficult to support their children financially during the two years of 'A' level study).

- *Rebels Without a Cause? Middle Class Youth and the Transition from School to Work* (1987) by Peter Aggleton: an ethnographic study of 27 'A' level students at a further education college in Bath. The students came from new middle-class backgrounds and under-achieved at 'A' level. They viewed themselves as belonging to a cultural élite and placed a high value on 'effortless achievement'. They were 'rebels' in the sense of wearing unconventional clothes, imitating Somerset 'yokel' accents, arriving at the dole office in a taxi, and refusing to conform to mainstream norms. 15 of the 27 students left the college without gaining any further qualifications, but six years later – at a time of high unemployment – they were all in full-time paid employment (e.g. as video technicians, servers in cocktail bars, arts assistants, etc.). Correspondence theorists point to the 'fit' between the students' class background, the value they placed on 'creative autonomy', and the 'niche' middle-class work roles they eventually came to occupy.

7% = 25%

- *A Class Act. The Myth of Britain's Classless Society* (1997) by Andrew Adonis and Stephen Pollard: in 1969 38% of places at Oxford University went to privately educated children and in the 1990s this had increased to around 50%. (Private schools only account for 7% of the total school population.) 'To complete the picture, a third of Etonians in 1996 were sons of Etonians.' Some 25% of all university entrants went to private schools. In 1995 more than 120 of 180 new officers who passed out of Sandhurst were privately educated. 'Private schools in the 1990s boast theatres, orchestras, language facilities and science labs superior to those of many universities.' In 1994 only 79 pupils from all the state secondary schools in the London borough of Islington were entered for two or more 'A' levels. Eton regularly sends between seventy and eighty of its pupils to Oxbridge.

- *Can school improvement overcome the effects of disadvantage?* (1997) by Peter Mortimore and Geoff Whitty argued there is a 'strong negative correlation' between social disadvantage and school achievement – indeed 'it would be odd if having warmer, more spacious accommodation, more nutritious food, better health, greater access to books, educational toys and stimulating experiences, and more informed knowledge about how the system works, did not confer considerable advantage in any tests or examinations.'

5 | Gender and education

- No female students were accepted by British universities until 1877. Females were not allowed to take degrees at London University until 1878 and at Oxford University until 1920. They were not admitted to full membership of Cambridge University until 1948. At the turn of the century it was common for boys and girls to be separated at the age of 7 and to follow different curricula.

- Under the post-1944 tripartite system girls achieved higher average scores than boys in the 11 plus examination. But in order to ensure that half the grammar school places were taken up by boys the scores were 'weighted' and girls' scores were marked down.

- Until the early 1970s males were more successful at 'O' / GCSE level than females, and until the early 1990s males were more successful at 'A' levels than females. Both patterns have since been reversed. Until 1997 a majority of university students were female. This pattern has since been reversed. Male university students still achieve higher results than female university students. Over 80% of university professors are male, and it will be some time before this is reversed.

- Men take the majority of degree places in science and engineering subjects. The male image of science is seen as putting females off, and there are few role-models of female scientists. Females who attend single-sex schools achieve better science results than females who attend co-educational schools.

- Boys are almost four times more likely than girls to have behavioural problems at school. Research on male educational under-achievement has focused on gender stereotypes. While girls are exposed to 'the image of woman as organiser', boys receive 'macho', anti-authority images of males enjoying the 'active company of other males', Jane Clarke, 'Gender and education revisited', *Sociology Review*, April 1996.

- 'It is not uncommon to ask teachers whether they give more attention to one sex than the other, and to have them vehemently protest that they do not . . . . But when their next lesson is taped it is often found that over two-thirds of their time was spent with the boys who comprised less than half of the class', Dale Spender, *Invisible Women: The Schooling Scandal* (1982).

> Gender patterns are fluid, not static!

6 | Ethnicity and education

- The Swann Report, *Education For All* (1985) found some improvement in the educational performance of ethnic minority children, but attainment levels of pupils of West Indian origin were significantly below those of white and Asian pupils. One group of Asian pupils – the Bangladeshis – did particularly badly at school. Educational under-achievement was explained in terms of:

  1 **Class background** (e.g. a high proportion of children of Bangladeshi origin lived in poverty).

  2 **Negative labelling:** racial prejudice at school contributed to under-achievement.

  3 **Family structure and cultural patterns:** (Asian pupils tended to 'keep their head down and adopt a low profile' in school, and a high proportion of their families were close-knit and supportive).

- Desmond Nuttall studied 30,000 pupils in Inner London and found that children of Indian origin did better than other groups at 'O' level and CSE, being ahead of Irish, English, Scottish, Welsh, Afro-Caribbean, and Bangladeshi children (quoted in Paul Trowler, *Investigating Education and Training* (1995)).

- D. Drew and J. Gray studied 14,500 pupils in England and Wales. 20% of all pupils, 19% of Asian pupils, and 7% of Afro-Caribbean pupils obtained five or more 'higher

> The Swann Report was the first systematic investigation of ethnicity and education.

grade' GCE/CSE passes. 51% of all pupils compared to 38% of Afro-Caribbean pupils achieved one or more 'higher grade' passes (quoted in *Investigating Education and Training* (1995)).

- D. J. Smith and S. Tomlinson in *The School Effect: A Study of Multiracial Comprehensives* (1989) studied 3,000 pupils in 20 schools. In 'the fourth and fifth years children belonging to ethnic minority groups tended to be allocated to lower course levels than children of UK origin.' However, schools with similar class and ethnic minority intakes differed in their academic performance, and the study concluded that '...what school a child goes to makes far more difference than which ethnic group he or she belongs to.'

- David Gilborn *'Race', Ethnicity and Education: Teaching and Learning in Multi-Ethnic Schools* (1990). Afro-Caribbean pupils in an inner-city comprehensive school were more likely than other pupils to be placed on detention. The teachers made a real attempt to treat all pupils fairly, but they interpreted (or misinterpreted) the dress and manner of speech of Afro-Caribbean pupils as representing a challenge to their authority.

- Department of Education figures for the early 1990s showed that Afro-Caribbean pupils were four times more likely to be permanently excluded from school than other pupils. (Possible explanations include: cultural misunderstandings; racial prejudice; social tensions gaining expression in deviant behaviour in the classroom.)

- *The Black Child Report* (1997) was based on interviews with 374 secondary school pupils of African and Afro-Caribbean descent. 15% thought they had been subjected to racism by a fellow pupil in the previous month, and nearly 40% said they would prefer to attend an all-black school.

- Over the last decade Afro-Caribbean girls have been staying on longer at school and achieving more academic success than black boys and white girls. Trevor Jones found that in 1988–90, 56% of minority ethnic children in the 16–19 age range were in full-time education compared with 37% of the white population, *Britain's Ethnic Minorities* (1993). In 1990, 9.6% of all admissions to higher education were from students of minority ethnic origin. (Only 6% of 18–24 year olds – the age-range of most applicants for higher education – have minority ethnic backgrounds.) A large number of voluntary Saturday schools have been established by black parents.

7 | Language and education

- L.S. Vygotsky (1896–1934) believed language was of vital significance for intellectual growth. Thought is a form of 'inner speech' and is not merely expressed in words but comes into existence through them.

- Basil Bernstein saw differential educational performance as partly explained by linguistic differences. Children from middle-class homes use the **elaborated code** – a complex and precise structure used by teachers at school. Children from working-class homes use the **restricted code** – shorter sentences and more context-bound; (containing assumptions which others are expected to know). The middle-class pupil experiences a continuity in language between home and school while the working-class child experiences a sharp discontinuity. Bernstein argued that unless schools respond more sensitively to this class gap in language use, considerable working-class talent will be wasted.

> Elaborated and restricted codes are key sociological concepts.

- Harold Rosen sees Bernstein's analysis as reflecting a class bias. It gives a stereotyped view of working-class language, and attributes intellectual virtues to middle-class speakers.

- William Labov researched Non-standard Negro English (NNE) amongst lower working-class black families in the USA. He rejected the view that they had a 'restricted' language code. In fact 'they hear more well-formed sentences than middle-class children, and participate fully in a highly verbal culture.'

8 | The Curriculum

- The **formal or official curriculum** consists of the subjects and course of study provided by schools. In 1988 the Government established a national curriculum for all students in state schools aged between 5 and 16. (Initially consisting of three core subjects – English, maths and science – and seven foundation subjects. There are four 'key stages' for different age groups: 5 to 7; 7 to 11; 11 to 14; and 14 to 16. Assessment takes place at the ages of 7, 11, 14, and 16.)

Examiners will expect you to be familiar with the hidden curriculum.

- In addition to the official curriculum a **hidden curriculum** of norms is taught implicitly in schools, e.g. unofficial 'subjects' such as 'punctuality', 'accepting authority', 'gender expectations', 'learning to be patient', 'getting on and fitting in with other people', 'wearing appropriate dress', etc. This hidden curriculum forms a fundamental part of school experience.

- The 'New' Sociology of Education applies a knowledge (or **epistemological**) perspective to study the school curriculum. (The 'Old' Sociology of Education focuses on the relationship between educational attainment and social background.) Key issues raised are who controls knowledge, and why some forms of knowledge are defined as worth learning at school but not others.

- M.F.D. Young drew a distinction between **high- and low-status knowledge**. High-status knowledge is: written rather than spoken; individualistic (both in the process of learning and in the presentation of what is learned); theoretical and abstract (unrelated to daily life and common experience). Low-status knowledge is: practical and applied; relates to everyday life; involves oral and group work.

The sociology of knowledge investigates the ranking of subjects as high-status 'academic' and low-status 'vocational'.

- According to Basil Bernstein high-status knowledge involves strong **framing** (the learners have no control over what is taught, how it is taught, or when it is taught) and strong **classification** (the boundaries of the subject are sharply drawn). Individuals from working-class backgrounds fail to achieve educational success because the high-status academic knowledge they encounter at school does not connect with their own cultural experience.

- Critics argue that some forms of knowledge have a higher status than others because they are of greater intellectual worth. If schools gave a lower priority to the teaching of high-status knowledge it would be even more difficult for working-class pupils to achieve upward mobility.

9 | Do schools make a difference?

- Christopher Jencks, *Inequality* (1972). Schools 'serve primarily as selection and certification agencies, whose job is to measure and label people, and only secondarily as socialisation agencies, whose job is to change people... schools serve primarily to legitimise inequality, not to make it.'

- W. Kenneth Richmond, *Education and Schooling* (1975). The functionalist view was summed up as follows: 'Since the educational system is a sub-system of the social system, any major reforms must await major changes in the latter. In other words, the tail cannot wag the dog!'

- Ivan Illich, *Deschooling Society* (1973) and Paulo Freire, *Pedagogy of the Oppressed* (1972). Both see schools as having a negative impact on society. They grade and degrade, reinforce status inequality, produce fatalism and conformity, and consolidate the structure of a repressive society. Schools should be replaced by 'learning webs' and attendance should be on a voluntary basis. Most people 'acquire most of their insight, knowledge and skill outside of school.'

- *The Bennett Report* (1976) compared different teaching methods (e.g. formal and informal) in primary schools. The experience and the professional commitment of the teacher, not the particular method used, was the key determinant of success.

- Michael Rutter *et al.*, *Fifteen Thousand Hours* (1979) studied twelve Inner London secondary schools. Attendance, behaviour at school, delinquency outside of school, and academic achievement were examined. Some schools were significantly more effective than others. A key factor was not the class background of the pupils but the 'ethos' (spirit or atmosphere) of the school and the professionalism of the teachers.

- Peter Mortimore *et al.*, *School Matters. The Junior Years* (1988). A study of 2,000 pupils (aged from 7 to 11) in 50 randomly selected primary schools in London. The school a child attends 'made a very important contribution to the explanation of variations in pupils' attainment and progress over three years in reading, writing and mathematics… and also to the development of attitudes, self-concept and behaviour in school.' To the question 'do junior schools make a difference to pupils' educational outcomes?' the study concluded: 'It is clear that schools do make a difference and that the difference is substantial.'

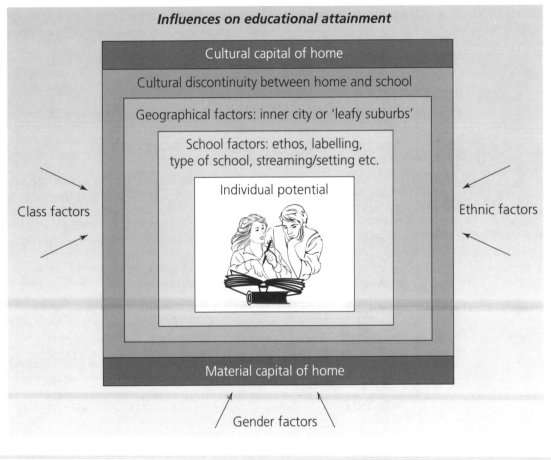

Influences on educational attainment

Cultural capital of home

Cultural discontinuity between home and school

Geographical factors: inner city or 'leafy suburbs'

School factors: ethos, labelling, type of school, streaming/setting etc.

Individual potential

Class factors

Ethnic factors

Material capital of home

Gender factors

- Pupils from private fee-paying schools achieve a high level of academic success with 88% going on to higher education compared with 27% of state school leavers. Some 46% of students at Oxbridge attended private schools, although only around 10% of pupils of secondary school age attend private schools. In the *Financial Times* 1997 league table of the top 1,000 schools for A-level performance, there was no state school in the top 70. Traditional élites (such as the judiciary, top civil servants, admirals, generals and air vice marshals) continue to be mainly composed of individuals from public school backgrounds. However, researchers argue that it is family background rather than the effect of attending a private school which is the key factor determining academic and career success (see Debra Roker 'Girls in Private Schools', *Sociology Review*, November 1994).

10 | Compensatory education

In the 1960s and 1970s compensatory education was a key social policy initiative.

- Supporters of **compensatory education** claim that schools can act as levers to compensate for social disadvantage.

- The Plowden Report, *Children and Their Primary Schools* (1967), proposed the introduction of positive discrimination with extra help given to schools in poor areas. The Report led to the establishment of Educational Priority Areas (EPAs), and some £16 million was made available by Government. Compensatory education was initiated in the USA in 1951, and a major 'Headstart' programme (which included high-quality nursery education) was launched in the USA in 1965. (The terms *affirmative action* and *reverse discrimination* are USA alternatives to the term compensatory education.)

- According to A.H. Halsey, individuals who attended Headstart were less likely to become unemployed or commit crime. However, in the 1980s programmes of compensatory education were largely abandoned.

- Critics on the left (e.g. Basil Bernstein) argued that 'education cannot compensate for society' and that policies of large-scale wealth and income redistribution were needed for the life-chances of socially disadvantaged children to be significantly improved. Critics on the right argued that the outcomes of compensatory education were too modest to justify their cost.

11 | Vocational education

In the 1980s and 1990s vocational education has been a key social policy initiative.

- In October 1976 the Labour Prime Minister James Callaghan made his 'Great Debate' speech at Ruskin College, Oxford. Teachers, he argued, must do more to meet the requirements of industry. **New vocationalism** refers to the various initiatives in education and training that were introduced by governments from 1974 on.

- In 1974 the Manpower Services Commission was established with responsibility for improving vocational training and education. It's now known as the Training, Enterprise and Education Directorate (TEED).

- A six-month Youth Opportunities Programme (YOP) was introduced in 1978 and then replaced by a one-year Youth Training Scheme (YTS) in 1983 (extended to two years in 1986). In 1990 this was replaced by Youth Training (YT), organised by Training and Enterprise Councils (TECs).

- The Technical and Vocational Educational Initiative (TVEI) introduced in 1980 gave financial support to schools which developed work-related courses for 14–19 year olds.

- In 1986 the National Council for Vocational Qualifications (NCVQ) was set up with the aim of introducing a coherent framework of vocational study. National Vocational Qualifications (NVQ) are specific to particular occupations, while General National Vocational Qualifications (GNVQ) consist of broader taught courses.

- City Technology Colleges (CTCs) were established from 1988 and are schools for 11 to 18 year olds with an emphasis on developing skills in mathematics, science, and technology.

- Supporters of the *new vocationalism* claim it will: raise the status of vocational training; develop transferable skills for use in a variety of occupations; make the labour force more adaptable; and upgrade the quality of human capital (the overall level of expertise in the population).

Examiners will expect you to be familiar with the debate on the New Vocationalism.

- Critics of the *new vocationalism* claim that: 'training' is a disguised form of cheap labour for employers; provides a means of 'massaging' unemployment statistics; keeps potentially troublesome youths off the streets; training programmes have generally been low quality; the labour force has been 'de-skilled' rather than 're-skilled'; despite Lord Young's belief (Employment Minister in the 1980s) that the two-year YTS qualification would come to be seen as 'equivalent to two 'A' levels' the status gap between academic and vocational qualifications remains as wide as ever.

12 | Checklist of key terms and concepts

Marketisation   State ideological apparatus   Role-allocation   Correspondence Theory
Self-fulfilling prophecy   Habitus   Cultural capital   Elaborated code   Restricted code
Hidden curriculum   Framing and classification   Compensatory education   Positive discrimination   New Vocationalism

13 | Further reading

Heaton, T. and Lawson, T. (1996) *Education and Training*, Basingstoke, Macmillan.

Lee, D. (1990) *Scheming for Youth*, Milton Keynes, Open University Press.

Mackinnon, D., Statham, J. and Hales, M. (1995) *Education in the UK: Facts and Figures*, London, Hodder and Stoughton.

Trowler, P. (1995) *Investigation Education and Training*, London, Collins Educational.

Chapter twelve

Poverty, health and welfare

1 | Definitions of absolute and relative poverty

- *Absolute poverty* exists where individuals lack sufficient resources to maintain their health.

- *Relative poverty* exists where individuals' standard of living is significantly lower than that of other people. J.C. Kincaid defines poverty as 'an inability to achieve a standard of living allowing for self-respect, the respect of others, and for full participation in society', *Poverty and Equality in Britain. A Study of Social Security and Taxation* (1973).

2 | Key terms

- **Cycle of deprivation:** poor children who grow up in poor families, in turn have children who are deprived,

- **Poverty life-cycle:** people are more likely to experience poverty at particular times in their lives (i.e. in childhood, when married with children, and in old age).

- **Poverty line:** individuals with incomes below this line are officially defined as living in poverty.

- **Poverty trap:** where individuals are unable to escape from poverty (e.g. an unemployed person obtains a low-paid job, ceases to be eligible for benefits, and experiences a fall in post-tax income).

- **Reference group:** acts as a yardstick for comparison.

- **Relative deprivation:** experienced by individuals who are worse off than individuals in their reference group.

3 | Key studies of poverty

> Booth and Rowntree were pioneer investigators of poverty in Britain.

- *Life and Labour of the People in London* (Vol.1) (1889) by Charles Booth. Booth, a wealthy ship owner, initially believed the problem of poverty to be exaggerated but then found that 31% of the population of London was living in poverty.

- *Poverty. A Study of Town Life* (1899) by Seebohm Rowntree. Rowntree, a wealthy chocolate manufacturer, initially believed that the numbers living in poverty in London were untypical of the country as a whole. Poor people were defined as those unable 'to maintain health and working efficiency'. Rowntree based his definition of the minimum diet needed by a family on the diets provided for Scottish prisoners (e.g. including one egg for the family per week). Rowntree found that 33% of York's population were living in poverty.

> Peter Townsend is a leading contemporary investigator of poverty.

- *The Poor and the Poorest* (1965) by Brian Abel-Smith and Peter Townsend. When this study was carried out it was widely believed that poverty had disappeared. (In Rowntree's final survey of poverty in York in 1950 he found that the percentage of the population in poverty had shrunk to 1.5%. Poverty in the late 19th-century sense – large-scale destitution and the workhouse – was gone.) The poor were first defined as those with incomes at or below the State's Social Security minimum. In 1960 3.8% of the population were found to be poor. When the yardstick of poverty was raised to 40% above the Social Security minimum (to include those living on the 'brink' of poverty) 14.2% of the population were found to be poor.

- *Poverty: The Forgotten Englishman* (1970) by Ken Coates and Richard Silburn. Based on a study of the inner-city St. Anne's district of Nottingham. Individuals with incomes of up to 40% above the Social Security minimum were defined as poor. 36% of the area's population were within this category. The main groups in poverty were: 1. pensioners; 2. low-income earners; 3. lone-parent families; 4. the chronically sick; 5. the unemployed.

- *Poverty in the United Kingdom* (1979) by Peter Townsend. Based on a national survey of 2,052 households in 1968–69. A 'deprivation index' was constructed based on such factors as not having a week's holiday away from home over the previous year, and not having a fridge. Poverty was defined as lacking sufficient financial resources to join in 'ordinary living patterns, customs and activities.' 22.9% of the population were found to be living in poverty.

- *Breadline Britain* (1983 and 1990) by Joanna Mack and Stewart Lansley. From a list of items (such as having a refrigerator, an indoor toilet, etc.) interviewees were asked to select those they felt were 'necessities'. The poor were defined as those who could not afford 3 or more necessities. In 1983 one in seven of the population were estimated to be living in poverty. The study was repeated in 1990 when the numbers in poverty were estimated to have increased to one in five of the population.

- *Inquiry into Income and Wealth* (1995) by the Joseph Rowntree Foundation defined the poor as those living on less than 50% of average income. On this definition in 1993 25% of the population were living in poverty compared with 9% in 1979. Changes in taxation, the increase in lone parents, falls in the real value of benefits, and increased unemployment had contributed to a growth in inequality and poverty.

4 | Criticisms of definitions of poverty

- There is no agreed definition of poverty. Even definitions of absolute poverty involve subjective judgements of what is needed to maintain health and what 'health' actually is. The numbers found to be 'poverty' can be increased or decreased by changing the poverty line.

- If poverty is defined in terms of social-security benefit rates, a government decision to increase the real value of benefits will simultaneously increase the numbers deemed to be living in 'poverty'. A government decision to lower the real value of benefits will simultaneously decrease the numbers deemed to be living in 'poverty'. Some researchers have defined poverty as an income of up to 40% above the social security minimum. But why not 50% above or 5% below?

- Some definitions of poverty are based on the concept of 'social participation' – the poor are unable to take part in 'ordinary living patterns, customs and activities.' But critics claim that redefining 'poverty' as lack of participation is to radically change the meaning of the term. Individuals have different tastes and some may not wish to participate in 'ordinary living patterns'.

- Some relative definitions of poverty use the concept of reference group. An individual experiences relative deprivation if those in his / her reference group are significantly better off. But this would mean that a millionaire whose reference group consisted of billionaires could be said to suffer from relative deprivation.

- Some definitions equate poverty with inequality. In Society X everyone is starving and everyone has the same economic assets – one slice of bread. In Society Y one half of the population have incomes of £50,000 a year and one half of the population have incomes of £500,000 a year. Relative poverty would exist in Society Y but not in Society X.

5 | The Welfare State

The Beveridge Report laid the foundations of the Welfare State in 1942. Welfare and warfare seem to accompany each other!

- The term *Welfare State* first appeared in print in 1941. It means that the government is responsible for providing a minimum level of tax-financed support for citizens in need. Before the Welfare State government policy was dominated by a *laissez-faire* philosophy. The Welfare State removes a sphere of life from the operation of market forces and thereby introduces **decommodification**. This occurs where 'a service is rendered as a matter of right, and when a person can maintain a livelihood without reliance on the market', Gosta Esping-Andersen, *The Three Worlds of Welfare Capitalism* (1990). Some theorists wish to rename the Welfare State the 'social investment state'.

- In 1942 the Beveridge *Report on Social Insurance and Allied Services* was published with the aim of creating a modern Welfare State and defeating the 'five giants' of want (poverty), idleness (unemployment), ignorance (lack of education), squalor (poor housing), and disease (poor health).

- Both the Labour Government of 1945–51 and the Liberal Government of 1906–14 helped establish the Welfare State. Key legislation included: **1908 Old Age Pensions Act**; **1911 National Insurance Ac**t (Part 1 introduced sickness benefit and free medical services; Part 2 introduced unemployment benefit); **1946 National Insurance Act** (provided the 'Beveridge Floor' of pension, unemployment and sickness benefits); **1946 National Health Service Act**; **1948 National Assistance Act** (set a 'Plimsoll' line of minimum income support below which no citizen would fall).

- The origins of the Welfare State can be traced back to the 1601 Poor Law Act which placed responsibility for caring for the poor in the hands of local government. Discontent amongst middle-class taxpayers about the cost of welfare eventually led to the passing of the 1834 Poor Law Amendment Act which introduced the principle of 'less eligibility'. This meant that the poor could no longer receive assistance in their own homes but had to enter the workhouse where conditions were deliberately made 'less eligible' – more unpleasant – than the conditions of life experienced by the lowest paid labourer.

Citizenship is a key concept in sociology and politics.

- A major component of the Welfare State is the National Health Service (NHS). This was founded in 1948 to provide free and universal health care. Its administrative structure was reorganised in 1974 and Area Health Authorities were abolished. During the 1980s and 1990s a number of 'market-led' reforms were introduced.

- The concept of *citizenship* (developed by T.H. Marshall (1893–1982)) strongly influenced the development of the modern Welfare State. The three components of citizenship are: civil (e.g. freedom of speech and access to the law); political (e.g. the right to vote); social (e.g. the right to welfare and security).

6 | The Left critique of the Welfare State

- The Welfare State has failed to significantly redistribute resources from rich to poor, or even to tackle basic problems of homelessness and poverty. A modest redistribution of resources has occurred within the working class (e.g. from those who are employed to the unemployed, from those who are below pension age to those of pension age and above, from those who are well to those who are ill).

- Welfare regulations have been designed to reinforce labour discipline (e.g. people engaged in trade union disputes or who leave their jobs 'voluntarily' are denied benefits). In the 1980s (when unemployment was high and the power of organised labour weak) there was a shift away from **universalism** (benefits available to all citizens) to **selectivity** (benefits only available to a means-tested few). Former residents of psychiatric hospitals have been removed from institutions and placed in under-resourced 'care in the community'. Reductions in the value of the state pension has reduced the living standards of the vulnerable.

- A welfare state will be maintained (albeit in a more residual form) since it provides an ideological legitimisation for capitalism, and helps maintain a productive workforce.

- But the scope of *collective* provision will be increasingly scaled down. Responsibility for funding pensions, higher education, etc. will be shifted from the state to the individual. The result will be an increase in social and economic inequality.

- Political debates on welfare costs usually ignore the *hidden welfare state* which operates to the benefit of the privileged – whereby the children of the middle class gain most from public expenditure on higher education, middle-class housebuyers gain most from tax relief on mortgages, and middle-class commuters gain most from rail subsidies. *Fiscal* welfare (the distribution of tax allowances and tax rates) and *occupational* welfare (fringe benefits such as a company car) should be included in discussions about welfare state costs.

7 | The Right critique of the Welfare State

Will the affluent two-thirds pay taxes to support the non-affluent one-third?

- The Welfare State places considerable pressure on government finances and taxation. In 1993 Peter Lilley (Minister responsible for social security) suggested that a 'fiscal crisis' was in prospect: 'The underlying growth in social security will continue to exceed growth in the economy.'

- Between 1980 and 1990 there was a 20% increase (in real terms) in expenditure on the NHS. Drugs and hospital technology are increasingly expensive, and medical science ensures more people survive into old age. The more successful the health service becomes, the more public expectations of what it can and should deliver are raised.

- As society becomes more affluent increasing numbers of people wish to make their own arrangements for welfare provision. Some 12% of the population now have private health insurance. The majority of people prefer to live in their own private housing rather than be dependent on publicly funded council housing.

- The role of the Welfare State will be reduced because of political factors ('tax and spend' policies have become electorally unfashionable), economic factors (the combined financial costs of pensions, social security, the NHS, and education are too high), and cultural factors (society has become more individualistic and less supportive of the concept of collective provision).

David Marsland is a leading New Right theorist.

- David Marsland believes that the Welfare State has created a culture of dependency which has eroded the capacity of individuals to be self-reliant and independent, *Welfare or Welfare State?* (1996).

- Functionalists claim that poor people raise the status of those who are not poor and provide a source of emotional satisfaction to affluent people who give charity; they reinforce dominant norms by demonstrating the price of failure, Howard Gans, *The Positive Functions of Poverty, American Journal of Sociology*, vol.78, no.2. A Welfare State which abolished poverty would thus be 'dysfunctional'.

8 | Explanations of the causes of poverty

8.1 Individualistic

- Individuals bring poverty on themselves because they lack initiative and are lazy.

- The Welfare State has created a culture of dependency and increased the numbers in the population who expect to be supported by the state and the taxpayer.

- Governments should give out 'signals' that the benefit culture is to end and that 'Welfare Into Work' is the only effective way of eliminating poverty.

- Critics argue that substantial groups in the population (such as the old, and the chronically sick and disabled) cannot move out of welfare into work. While some benefit claimants may prefer not to work (perhaps 15%) the great majority are trapped by circumstances they cannot control.

8.2 Cultural

- A classic cultural study was *La Vida* (1967) by Oscar Lewis. Lewis saw poverty in sub-cultural terms, as a way of life passed down from generation to generation. 'By the time slum children are aged six or seven they usually have absorbed the basic values and attitudes of their subculture and are not psychologically geared to take full advantage of changing conditions or increased opportunities which may occur in their lifetime.' Poverty is 'not only a matter of economic deprivation' but is also 'something positive, and provides some rewards without which the poor could hardly carry on.'

- Although Lewis is sympathetic to the poor, there are similarities between his concept of the culture of poverty and the tough-minded New Right culture of dependency concept. Both think 'fatalism and a low level of aspiration is one of the key traits of the subculture of poverty.'

- Critics see both cultural explanations of poverty as putting the cart before the horse: the fatalistic culture of the poor is a response to economically adverse conditions, not its cause.

> Lewis sees the culture of poverty as having positive functions.

8.3 Structural

- Poverty is a product of economic circumstances. Inequality in the distribution of economic resources, and the resulting powerlessness for those at the bottom, inevitably leads to poverty.

- Middle-class individuals who join the ranks of the long-term unemployed start to show 'culture of poverty' symptoms.

- The 'expressive' style of slum life is a logical response to economic disadvantage. By making themselves appear interesting and dramatic, individuals increase the likelihood of obtaining some of the few rewards that are available.

- The growth of poverty in Britain since the 1970s is only explicable in structural and economic terms. Unemployment has increased sharply; the labour market has become more casualised; the real value of pensions and other benefits has fallen; inequality in the distribution of wealth and income has grown.

- Critics see structural explanations as refusing to acknowledge that once a culture of poverty or a culture of dependency has come into existence, it is a real barrier to individual self-advancement.

> Examiners will expect you to be able to compare and contrast structural, cultural and individualistic explanations of poverty.

9 | Health

9.1 Definition

- The World Health Organisation puts forward a **positive definition of health** as 'not merely the absence of disease and infirmity but complete physical, mental and social well-being.' Most people have a **negative definition of health**, which refers to the absence of illness.

9.2 Trends in health

- Nicky Hart, *The Sociology of Health and Medicine* (1985), points out: 'Before 1900, infective diseases like tuberculosis accounted for most deaths [in Britain] at every age, yet today they have virtually disappeared. Their place has been taken by accidents among young people and by heart disease and cancer among middle aged and older people. The elimination of fatal infections has been associated with a 'leap forward' in life expectation. More than 60% of the total decline [in mortality] between 1850 and 1970 was due to a reduction in infective conditions. measles, scarlet fever, pneumonia, bronchitis, whooping cough – all declined. Hospitals did not make an appreciable impact on health in the 19th century. Latrogenic conditions – sickness brought about by medical treatment itself – were widespread.'

9.3 The problem of health statistics

- Over 90% of illness is not reported to doctors. Official statistics of morbidity (illness) only represent the visible part of a 'clinical iceberg'. Doctors – who act as 'gatekeepers' in defining whether someone can legitimately claim sickness or invalidity benefit – differ in their willingness to classify individuals as being 'ill'. Doctors and coroners differ in their judgements of causes of death (mortality).

9.4 Theoretical perspectives on health

- **Functionalists** like Talcott Parsons point out that by taking on the 'sick role' individuals acquire certain 'rights' (such as exemption from work and everyday pressures and responsibilities). But the sick role carries 'obligations' as well: individuals must appear to comply with their doctor's advice and show that they wish to get better and are 'genuinely' ill.

- **Marxists** see doctors as state agents of social control: they decide who is unable (and who is unwilling) to work. Marxists believe that some of the highly profitable products of drugs companies distributed by the health service damage patients' health, and that the state has turned a blind eye to various profitable practices which threaten public health (e.g. the manufacture of tobacco, the over-use of fertilisers in farming, and conditions in abattoirs).

- **Interactionists** have focused on the damaging effects of the stigmatised labels imposed on sick people. Also, some medical treatment can actually make people ill (*iatrogenesis*).

- **Feminists** point out that senior positions in the medical profession are dominated by men who subscribe to a *bio-mechanical model of health* (the body is a defective machine which has to be repaired). Women have been disempowered from taking control over their own bodies and health processes.

- **Post-modernists** see professional medical knowledge (and the bio-mechanical model of health on which it is based) as legitimising domination. They question the superiority of the 'scientific narrative'. The growing popularity of complementary medicine reflects individuals' desire to take more control of their own health rather than being dependent on alleged 'experts'.

9.5 Inequalities in health and illness

- According to the 'inverse care law' medical and health care resources are distributed in inverse proportion to need. Those in greatest need get fewest resources, whilst those in least need get most resources. Thus the most run-down and overcrowded NHS facilities are found in working-class areas, J.Tudor-Hart 'The Inverse Care Law', *The Lancet* (27.2.71).

- The Black Report, *Report of the Working Party on Inequalities in Health* (1980), and *The Health Divide* (1987 and 1992) found that the risk of mortality and morbidity was significantly higher for lower occupational classes. In 1984 'babies whose fathers had unskilled jobs ran approximately twice the risk of stillbirth and death under one year than babies whose fathers worked in the professions.' Between 1971 and 1981 'non-manual groups experienced a much greater decline in death rates than manual groups, thus the gap between the two groups widened.' Rates of obesity are higher in lower social groups, survival rates from cancer and coronary heart disease are lower, fewer people in the lower social groups retain their natural teeth, and they are likely to be of lower height than people in the 'higher' social groups.

- Studies have found that working-class patients are given shorter periods of consultation with their doctors than middle-class patients.

- Jeanette Mitchell, *What is to be done about illness and health?* (1984) points out that according to the General Household Survey: 'Four times as many women die of cervical cancer in Class 5 as in Class 1. The prevalence of chronic depression was found to be 5 times greater among working-class women compared with middle class women. The babies of Class 1 mothers are half as likely to die within the first week of life as the babies of people at the bottom of society... A quarter of the children who die between the ages of 5 and 9 are killed by motor vehicles, and this is 6 times more likely to happen to children in Class 5... Shiftwork has been shown to give rise to nervous disorders, digestive problems and ulcers. Living in flats carries a higher risk of accidents and depression. Infant mortality rates are higher in overcrowded housing and homes with shared bathrooms and toilets.'

- The life expectancy for males in professional occupations is seven years higher than for men in unskilled manual work. Although there has been a general increase in life expectancy, statistics published by the Office for National Statistics in 1997 show there has actually been a small *decline* in life expectancy for unskilled and semi-skilled manual workers. They also reveal that 'life expectancy for a boy born in Cambridge is now 76 years and seven months compared with a boy born in Manchester for whom it is 69 years and 11 months', *Sociology Update 1998*.

- Females have lower infant mortality rates than males, and their life expectancy is six years higher. However, females have higher rates of admission to psychiatric hospitals than males, are more likely to be registered as disabled, are more than twice as likely to be in hospital, and make more visits to their doctor.

- Individuals of Afro-Caribbean and Asian origin are more likely to be admitted to psychiatric hospitals (for both voluntary and compulsory admissions). They have higher rates of mortality than the white population (as a result of greater exposure to social disadvantage). Some diseases (such as sickle cell anaemia amongst Afro-Caribbean individuals and cystic fibrosis in the white population) are associated with ethnicity.

9.6 Explanations of inequalities in health and illness

- **The artefact explanation:** 'inequalities' are a statistical illusion. Unskilled manual workers tend to be older than workers in other classes, which is why their mortality and morbidity rates are higher. The number of unskilled workers has declined significantly in recent decades. Critics of this explanation claim 'there can be no doubt that these inequalities exist however imperfect the measuring tool', *The Health Divide* (1987).

- **The social selection explanation:** inequalities do exist, but simply reflect the fact that 'survival of the fittest' means that those who are healthy tend to be upwardly mobile while those who are unhealthy tend to be downwardly mobile. Critics acknowledge that some evidence supports this view (e.g. tall women are more likely to be upwardly mobile than short women). However, the explanation 'accounts for only a small proportion of the overall differential between the social classes' *The Health Divide* (1987).

- **The cultural/behavioural explanation:** inequalities do exist, but these reflect life-style choices. *The Health Divide* reported that heavy drinking is much more common among manual workers; high income groups consume more fresh fruit and vegetables; there has been very little reduction in smoking amongst working-class women; unskilled workers have the lowest participation in walking and swimming while professionals have the highest. Critics claim that health-damaging behaviour and differences in lifestyles only account for 25% of class inequalities in health.

- **The structuralist/materialist explanation:** health inequalities reflect economic inequalities. The risks of accidents in the workplace are far greater in manual than in professional occupations. Poor housing is associated with a higher risk of domestic accidents. Damp housing causes health problems. Unsafe play areas increase the likelihood of accidents to children. A healthy diet could cost up to 35% more than the typical diet of a low-income family. *The Health Divide* concludes that 'socio-economic circumstances' are an important source of health inequalities.

10 | Checklist of key terms and concepts

Absolute and relative poverty   Cycle of poverty and poverty life-cycle   Reference group
Decommodification   The 'five giants'   Less eligibility   The hidden welfare state
Fiscal and occupational welfare   Civil, political, and social rights of citizenship
Universalism and Selectivity   Culture of poverty and culture of dependency
The clinical iceberg   Latrogenesis   The bio-mechanical model of health
Inverse Care Law

11 | Further reading

Aggleton, P. (1990) *Health*, London, Routledge.

Cole, T. (1996) *Whose Welfare?*, London, Tavistock.

Oppenheim, C. and Harker, L. (1996) *Poverty: The Facts*, 3rd edition, London, Child Poverty Action Group.

Trowler, P. (1996) *Investigating Health Welfare and Poverty*, London, Collins Educational.

Chapter thirteen

Work, leisure and unemployment

1 | Work

- Work consists of 'the supply of physical, mental, and emotional effort to produce goods and services for own consumption, or for consumption by others', *The Concise Oxford Dictionary of Sociology* (1994).

- Work is performed in:

- The *formal economy*: the official economy or paid employment.

- The *informal economy*: the unofficial economy (e.g. working for friends in return for services).

- The *household economy*: domestic labour (e.g. housework and child care).

- The *communal economy*: voluntary work outside the domestic sphere, Ray Pahl, *Divisions of Labour* (1984).

- The **self-service economy**: individuals provide services for themselves, e.g. driving a car rather than travelling by bus, watching a video rather than going to the cinema, Jonathan Gershuny, *After Industrial Society? Emerging Self Service Economy* (1978).

2 | Industrial society

- *The Industrial Revolution* (1760–1850) transformed the nature of work. It involved a breakthrough in the use of inanimate energy and power (especially steam power); massive investment in industries such as iron, coal, and textiles and a transport revolution (first canals, then railways). By 1851 the majority of the population – for the first time in history – was living in cities.

- Industrialisation changed the time dimension of work. In pre-industrial society work was **task-oriented**, while in industrial society it is **time-oriented**. In industrial society 'those who are employed experience a distinction between their employer's time and their "own" time. And the employer must use the time of his labour, and see it is not wasted... Time is now currency: it is not passed but spent', E.P. Thompson *Time, Work Discipline and Industrial Capitalism, Past and Present*, vol. 38, 1967.

- *The Industrial Revolution* was the *second wave* of change in history. The *first wave* took place 10,000 years ago when agriculture first developed. A *third wave* of change is now taking place and a *post-industrial/ knowledge/ information/ technetronic society* is emerging. Those who produce and process information will form a majority of the labour force.

> *Sociology was a product of the Industrial Revolution!*

> *Alvin Toffler coined the term the 'third wave'.*

3 | Defining leisure

- Leisure consists of activities which people choose to do in their free time. It is a sphere of life not occupied in work, travelling to work, or in routine domestic responsibilities.

- **Segmentalists** argue that it is possible to compartmentalise and separate the sphere of work from the sphere of leisure. **Holists** argue that individuals' lives cannot be split up, and that the attitudes developed in one segment of life inevitably spill over into another.

- Joffre Dumazedier views leisure as having two central characteristics:

> *Are you a segmentalist or a holist?*

1 it is the result of free choice and is done as an end in itself;

2 it involves a search for personal fulfilment, contentment, and pleasure.

- Stanley Parker refers to a continuum, with 'sold time' (paid employment) at one end and 'choosing time' (leisure) at the other. Parker refers to three patterns of work–leisure relationship. 1. **Extension:** taking place in occupations which have high levels of job satisfaction; there is no sharp distinction between work and leisure; work-related activities are carried over into leisure time. 2. **Opposition:** taking place in occupations which have low levels of job satisfaction; there is a sharp distinction between work and leisure; activities are deliberately chosen which are different from those of work. 3. **Neutrality:** taking place in occupations where work is neither satisfying enough to be carried over into leisure, nor so unfulfilling that leisure is sought as a compensation.

- Rhona and Robert Rapoport show how choice of leisure activities varies with the stage reached in the life-cycle. The four main stages are: adolescence (approximately 15–19); young adulthood (20–25); the 'settling down' / establishment phase (26–55); the later years (56+).

- Kenneth Roberts believes that trends in leisure have led to an increase in both home-centredness (television 'has strengthened the home's position as most people's main leisure centre') and out-of-home recreation (e.g. tourism and use of sport and leisure centres). Connoisseur leisure will continue to expand (e.g. the arts, the countryside, wines). Unemployed and poor sections of the population will express their resentment at being excluded from the 'leisure society' by engaging in crime and unruly behaviour in public places.

- Between 1980 and 1996 men's earnings rose by 214% and women's by 259%. A. Adonis and S. Pollard note that this rise in disposable incomes has not changed the class character of leisure. 'Every sport has its class labels. Ascot is for toffs, the Grand National for 'the people'', *A Class Act. The Myth of Britain's Classless Society* (1997).

- According to historical research as much as a third of the year in the Middle Ages was devoted to leisure.

So much for progress!

- **Functionalists** see leisure as providing an escape from the monotony of work: it is a 'reward' for role-conformity and enables people to unwind and adjust to their life situation. **Marxists** point to the commercial exploitation of leisure: alienated individuals exploited at work become alienated leisure-seekers exploited at play. **Weberians** note how leisure in industrial societies has been increasingly subjected to bureaucratic regulation and rationalisation (e.g. the change in football from spontaneous mass kick-about to rule-bound spectator sport). **Interactionists** and **pluralists** emphasise the variety of experience and meaning which different people derive from leisure. **Feminists** note that the relationship between leisure and housework has been largely ignored by research, and that male control over the public sphere (such as the streets at night and public houses) limits female leisure opportunities. **Post-modernists** refer to how leisure enables individuals to redefine and reconstruct their personal identities.

4 | Alienation

- 'Alienation is derived from the Latin *alienare* to estrange or make another's; and relates to *alienus* (belonging to another person or place).... From the 15th century on it has been used to describe the action of transferring the ownership of anything to another...The most widespread contemporary use is probably that derived from one form of psychology, a loss of connection with one's deepest feelings and needs', Raymond Williams, *Keywords* (1976).

- 'What, then, constitutes the alienation of labour? First, the fact that labour is external to the worker, i.e. it does not belong to his essential being; that in his work, therefore, he does not affirm himself but denies himself, does not feel content but unhappy… His labour is therefore not voluntary, but coerced; it is forced labour', Karl Marx, *Economic and Philosophic Manuscripts of 1844*.

- 'Alienated labour has four aspects to it. Firstly, the worker was related to the product of his labour as an alien object… Secondly, the worker became alienated from himself in the very act of production; for the worker did not view his work as part of his real life and did not feel at home in it. Thirdly, man's "species-life", his social essence, was taken away from him…Fourthly, man found himself alienated from other men', David McLellan, *Marx* (1975).

- Robert Blauner views alienation as four dimensions: powerlessness, meaninglessness, isolation, and self-estrangement. Research on workers in the printing, textiles, automobiles, and chemicals industries led him to formulate the Inverted U-curve Theory of Alienation, i.e. alienation is lowest in craft production (printing); increases significantly with factory production (textiles), reaches a peak with assembly line production (car workers), and falls with automation (chemicals), *Alienation and Freedom* (1964). Critics claim that Blauner's methodology was flawed (being partly based on research from 1947), and that he ignores both the ownership structure of industry and the cultural values which workers bring to the workplace. Other studies have challenged his view that workers in automated plants experience low levels of alienation (e.g. T. Nichols and H. Benyon, *Living With Capitalism* (1977)).

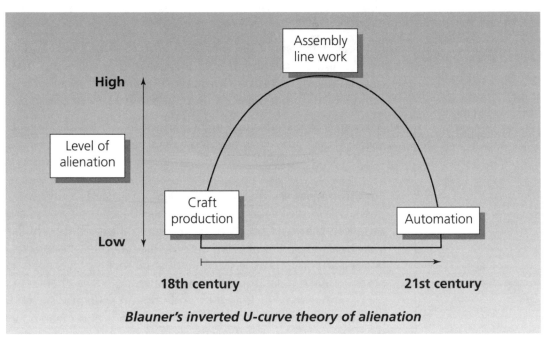

Blauner's inverted U-curve theory of alienation

- 'They all tell you the story about the man who left Ford to work in a sweet factory where he had to divide up the reds from the blues, but left because he couldn't take the decision-making… Continually Ford workers tell you "never buy a Ford". Neither is this peculiar to Ford…General Motors workers are reputed to have bought Fords instead of Chevrolets because they "knew how Chevrolets were built and would not advise anybody to buy one."' When a foreman was told that a worker had dropped dead on the assembly line it was said that his first response was to 'clock him out', i.e. make sure that he would not be paid for any minutes after he died, Huy Beynon, *Working For Ford* (1973).

- According to Ann Oakley the social isolation, time pressure, and monotony of housework generates a higher level of alienation than the factory assembly line. The 40 housewives in her sample spent an average of 77 hours a week on housework. One housewife interviewed said: 'When I was working I used to get a tremendous kick out of doing…housework. But now I'm doing it every day it really is the biggest bore of my life', *Housewife* (1976).

5 | Theories of work

5.1 Scientific management (or 'Taylorism').

Economic model of man versus social model of man.

- Developed by F. W. Taylor (1856–1915) who wrote *The Principles of Scientific Management* (1911). Taylor was a management consultant whose work study techniques produced a 400% increase in pig iron production in the Bethlehem steel works in the USA. Workers had attempted to slow down their production rates to keep pay rates high. Taylor countered this by placing complete control of the work process in the hands of management. He saw economic rewards and incentives as the key means of increasing productivity.

5.2 The Human Relations School

- Elton Mayo (1880–1949) rejected an *economic* model of man. According to his *social* model of man, individuals will become more productive if they work in an emotionally supportive environment and have more of a say in decision-making and responding to their social and group needs. Experiments Mayo carried out in the Hawthorne Works in Chicago revealed that non-economic factors – the presence of researchers in the factory – brought about an increase in productivity.

5.3 Theory X and Theory Y

- According to **Theory X** the average human being has an inherent dislike of work and will avoid it if s/he can. People must be coerced if their employers' goals are to be achieved. According to **Theory Y** the average human being has self-actualisation needs and seeks to fulfil these in work. The desire for personal growth rather than external threats is the key to work motivation.

- **Theory X** will be dominant in **low-trust systems** with conflict between workers and management and low job satisfaction. *Theory Y* will be dominant in **high-trust systems** with co-operation between workers and management, and high job satisfaction.

- **Theory X** is sometimes known as the 'rabble hypothesis', i.e. without an authoritarian system of control organisational goals will not be achieved.

5.4 Fordism and Post-Fordism

Fordism and Post-Fordism are key sociological concepts.

- **Fordism** is shorthand for the system of industrial production which was dominant in advanced industrial societies between the 1920s and 1970s. Standardised goods are produced for a mass market, and workers perform repetitive tasks within a rigid and hierarchical division of labour. Fordism is symbolised in the moving assembly line. This originated in Chicago slaughterhouses and was used from 1908 on in the car factories of Henry Ford (1863–1947).

- **Post-Fordism** is shorthand for a new system of industrial production which emerged in the early 1980s. High-quality products (rather than cheap mass-produced goods) are made in factories employing small numbers of specialist workers. Computer-aided design and manufacture (CAD/CAM) mean that a variety of 'niche' products can be manufactured. Henry Ford said customers can have any colour of car they like 'as long as it's black'. Post-Fordist customers can have any colour of car they want. Workers in Fordist factories had to mentally switch off and do what they were told. Workers in Post-Fordist factories can exercise some intellectual autonomy at work and experience a variety of tasks.

- Critics point out that some jobs in new sectors of the economy (such as fast-food chains) mix both Fordist and Post-Fordist features. An example would be a 'McJob' which Douglas Coupland defines as 'A low-pay, low-dignity, low-benefit, no-future job in the service sector. Frequently considered a satisfying career choice by people who have never had one', *Generation X. Tales For An Accelerated Culture* (1992).

6 | Technology and work

6.1 Technological determinism

- Factors which are intrinsic to the workplace are seen as having a decisive influence on behaviour at work and job satisfaction. Robert Blauner claims that assembly-line technology generates high levels of alienation and craft technology generates low levels of alienation. Convergence theorists believe that the imperatives of technology mean that all industrial societies (whether their ideology is 'capitalist' or 'communist') will become alike and have similar social structures.

6.2 Social determinism

- Factors which are extrinsic to the workplace have a decisive influence on behaviour at work and job satisfaction. A comparative study supporting this view was *In Search of the New Working Class. Automation and integration within the capitalist enterprise* (1978) by Duncan Gallie. This investigation of workers in four oil refineries (two in France and two in Britain) found that British workers had higher levels of job satisfaction and a less 'oppositional' political consciousness than French workers. Since they all operated the same automated technology these differences could only be explained in terms of extrinsic factors, i.e. differences in political culture. *The Affluent Worker* (1968) study in Luton also concluded that the attitudes the car workers brought to the workplace (rather than the technology in the workplace) were of critical significance.

6.3 Socio-technical approach

- This focuses on the interaction of both intrinsic and extrinsic factors. *Workers' Attitudes and Technology* (1976) by D. Weddernburn and R. Crompton studied a chemical complex in the north-east and found that strike and absenteeism rates were higher amongst machine shop workers than amongst continuous-process plant workers (whose work was less routine). The research concluded that levels of job satisfaction and behaviour at work are influenced by both technology and the subjective orientations which individuals bring to the workplace.

7 | Conflict at work

7.1 Forms of conflict

- **Strikes:** organised industrial action by employees.
- **Working to rule:** if rules and regulations are followed to the letter, productivity falls dramatically.
- **Sabotage:** employees inflict deliberate damage on their place of employment.
- **Absenteeism:** employees' discontent is manifested in feigning sickness.
- **Employer-initiated conflict includes:** lock-outs, 'plant closure, sackings, victimisation, blacklisting, speed-up, safety hazards, arbitrary discipline, and so on', R. Hyman, *Strikes* (1991).

> Examiners will expect you to be able to compare and contrast technological determinism and social determinism.

> Conflict can be initiated by employers or employees.

7.2 Strikes

Official statistics on strikes are problematic.

- A strike is a temporary stoppage of work by employees who seek to express a grievance or enforce a demand, Richard Hyman, *Strikes* (1991).

- Strike activity is measured in terms of: the number of strikes; the proportion of the labour force which participates in strikes; and the number of working days lost through strikes. Official statistics on strikes are incomplete. Strikes which last less than a full day, or involve fewer than ten workers, or are 'political' strikes, are excluded.

- In the 1970s there was a sharp increase in the number and duration of both official and unofficial strikes. Only during the turbulent years of industrial unrest following the 1914–18 war were strike levels significantly higher. Trade union membership peaked at 13.4 million in 1979 when 58% of the workforce belonged to unions. By 1997 union membership (according to the Labour Force Survey) had fallen to 7.1 million with under 31% of the workforce belonging to unions.

Since 1979 there has been a sharp decline in the number of trade unionists and a sharp increase in the number of shareholders.

- Apart from 1984 (when the miners' strike began) there has been a sharp decline in the number and duration of strikes. In the 1980s unions' bargaining power was weakened by the rise in unemployment. Job loss was particularly severe in heavy industry (which was highly unionised). Jobs expanded in the service sector where union organisation is traditionally weak and workers mainly female (who may well regard unions as bastions of male chauvinism). Laws were passed restricting and controlling union activity. The 1980 Employment Act removed legal protection from union members engaged in 'secondary action' (i.e. action at somewhere other than their own place of work). The 1984 Trade Union Act required all official strikes to be preceded by a secret ballot of union members.

7.3 Explanations of strikes

1 **Level of community integration.** Clark Kerr and Abraham Siegel – in A. Kornhauser *et al*. (eds) *Industrial Conflict* (1954) found that homogeneous and isolated occupational groups (such as miners, dockers, and lumbermen) had higher then average strike levels. There is a strong sense of community, promotion opportunities are few, and very limited alternative employment.

2 **Accumulated grievances.** Alvin Gouldner, *Wildcat Strikes* (1957), saw strikes as an emotional explosion of discontent which follows a long build-up of perceived injustices.

3 **Absence of negotiation machinery.** A.M. Ross and P.T.Hartman, *Changing Patterns of Industrial Conflict* (1960) saw the lack of Government conciliation machinery and established negotiation procedures as making strikes more likely to occur.

4 **Normal features of industrial life.** Tony Lane and Kenneth Roberts, *Strike at Pilkingtons* (1971), concluded that given the nature of alienated work, the framework of employer–employee relations, and the integration of trade union leaders into the power structure, gathering large numbers of workers together under one roof makes periodic outbreaks of unrest almost inevitable.

Examiners will expect you to be able to compare and contrast explanations of strikes.

5 **Strong bargaining position.** Workers who occupy a strategic position in the economy may use strikes to strengthen their bargaining position.

6 **A reflection of workplace characteristics.** W.W. Daniel and N. Millward, *Workplace Industrial Relations in Britain* (1983), higher strike rates are associated with a high proportion of full-time male workers; large firms; workplace rather than national bargaining, and agreed negotiating procedures between management and workers.

7 **No single factor.** Richard Hyman, *Strikes* (1991), strikes are inherently unpredictable. They are caused by specific circumstances in specific workplaces, and are influenced by a variety of cultural and economic factors, with chance and accidental factors playing a part.

8 | Unemployment

8.1 Types of unemployment

- **Frictional unemployment:** individuals who are changing jobs.

  Structural unemployment: individuals who have lost their jobs because of technological change.

  Cyclical unemployment: individuals who have lost their jobs because of ups and downs in the economic cycle (e.g. the recession of 1980–1983).

  Voluntary unemployment: individuals who choose not to work. (According to the 'sturdy beggar' hypothesis a minority of the unemployed choose not to seek work after having made a rational calculation of costs and benefits.)

8.2 Extent of unemployment

Official statistics on unemployment are 'problematic'.

- Official statistics on unemployment only date from 1914.

- In 1932 22% of the labour force was unemployed.

- Between 1948 and 1966 the average number of people registered as unemployed was just over 350,000 – less than 2% of the labour force. At this time it was widely believed that the growth in world trade and Keynesian steering of the economy (i.e. the government countering a deficit in demand by increasing public spending during periods of recession) had permanently ended mass unemployment.

- Unemployment reached 1 million in 1971 (the first time since the 1930s).

The 'long boom' of the post-war years ended in the 1970s.

- In 1983 over 3 million people (12.6% of the labour force) were registered as unemployed. Technological change; competition from newly industrialised countries; world economic recession and increased numbers of female workers entering the labour market had contributed to the growth in unemployment. New Right theorists claimed that: the work incentive had been eroded by welfare benefits, public expenditure had led to an increase in inflation, and wage rates had been pushed up too far by trade unions.

8.3 Measuring unemployment

The three main methods used are:

1 Counting the numbers who are claiming unemployment benefit. (Changes in regulations of eligibility for benefits can produce an artificial 'rise' or 'fall' in the numbers of unemployed. Between 1979 and 1987 there were nineteen changes in the official measurement of unemployment.)

2 Conducting surveys to find the numbers of individuals who are available for work and have been actively seeking employment over the previous month. (This is the measure used by the International Labour Organisation (ILO) and is the most widely accepted.)

3 Conducting surveys to find the numbers of individuals who are unemployed but have not been actively seeking employment because they do not believe any jobs are available. (This measure is used by the Unemployment Unit, which campaigns on behalf of the unemployed.)

8.4 Accuracy of unemployment statistics

- Official statistics underestimate the extent of unemployment since only those who are registered as unemployed are counted, and some groups (e.g. those on training schemes) are automatically excluded.

- To a lesser extent official statistics overestimate the extent of unemployment since they include those who choose not to work, and those who work in the 'black economy' while claiming benefits.

- Research by Ray Pahl has found that the majority of individuals working in the 'black economy' are also working in full-time jobs. Also, families tended to be either 'work-rich' (albeit 'time-poor') – both partners were working – or 'work-poor' (albeit 'time-rich') – with neither partner working.

8.5 Social distribution of unemployment

Patterns of unemployment reflect differences in life-chances.

- Rates of unemployment (including long-term unemployment) are highest amongst:
  - unskilled and semi-skilled manual workers;
  - some ethnic minority groups;
  - young people aged under 25 and old people aged over 50;
  - those living in particular regions (such as Northern Ireland and the North of England); and those living in inner city areas.
  - official statistics show that males have higher unemployment rates than females. However these underestimate the numbers of females who are unemployed (e.g. a high proportion of married women seeking employment are not eligible for unemployment benefit).

- *Note:* the unemployed are not a static group. Unemployment has been likened to a bath which is constantly being filled by the newly unemployed and constantly emptied by those who succeed in finding work, David Ashton, *Unemployment Under Capitalism* (1986).

8.6 Effects of unemployment

'Structured meaning' is an important sociological concept.

- Economic: fall in income and material living standards.

- Physical health: increased risk of morbidity.

- Psychological damage: four stages of unemployment have been identified:
  1 **shock**
  2 **denial and optimism**
  3 **anxiety and distress**
  4 **resignation and adjustment.** The classic study of the psychological effects of unemployment was carried out by M. Jahoda, P. Lazarfield and H. Zeisel, *Marienthal: The Sociography of an Unemployed Community* (1933). The unemployed became socially isolated, had high rates of divorce, and were likely to experience physical and mental illness (including suicide and parasuicide). Their lives lacked 'structured meaning' and they lost a sense of time; weekdays blurred into weekends and extra time was spent in bed. (Work provides a structure of time and a framework for social contacts.)

- **Economic and social costs:** the value of the goods and services the unemployed could have produced is lost; if unemployment is rising there is a loss in taxation revenue just when increased public expenditure is required to fund benefits; a rise in unemployment places greater pressure on the NHS (individuals who become unemployed are more likely to fall ill); family breakdown increases; the crime rate rises; outbreaks of social disorder become more common.

- *Interactionists* focus on how unemployment is subjectively perceived. Some individuals experience unemployment as a period of personal renewal, especially if they were previously in highly stressful employment.

9 | Checklist of key terms and concepts

The self-service economy   The Industrial Revolution   Task-oriented and time-oriented work   Post-industrial society   Segmentalists and Holists   Extension, opposition, and neutrality   Inverted U-curve Theory of Alienation   Theory X and Theory Y   Fordism and Post-Fordism   Technological determinism and social determinism   Convergence theory   Frictional unemployment   Structural unemployment   Cyclical unemployment   Structured meaning.

10 | Further reading

Crompton, R. (1997) *Women and Work in Modern Britain*, Oxford, Oxford University Press.

Deem, R. (1988) *Work, Unemployment and Leisure*, London, Routledge.

Grint, K. (1991) *The Sociology of Work: An Introduction*, Cambridge, Polity Press.

Madry, N. and Kirby, M. (1996) *Investigating Work, Unemployment and Leisure*, London, Collins Educational.

Chapter fourteen

Religion

1 Definition

'An attitude of awe towards God, or gods, or the supernatural, or the mystery of life, accompanied by beliefs and affecting basic patterns of individual and group behaviour. In Latin *religare* means "to bind", and religion is traditionally what most deeply binds a society...' – *The Fontana Dictionary of Modern Thought* (1977), edited by A. Bullock and O. Stallybrass.

- Durkheimian approaches focus on collective worship, religious practice, the effects of religious moral codes on behaviour, and the functions of religion.

- Weberian approaches focus on the subjective or phenomenological dimension of religion – on how religion provides meaning to individuals.

- Religion involves:
  1 collective forms of practice and worship;
  2 shared beliefs in the holy or sacred, the supernatural or superhuman.

- Note:

  1 Some religions are *monotheistic* (they believe in one god); some religions are *polytheistic* (they believe in many gods).

  2 One form of religion is **animism** – a belief in spirits or ghosts.

  3 **Religiosity** refers to the strength of religious beliefs and practices in a society.

  4 **Magic** is a kind of 'supernatural technology' which is seen as enabling people to intervene in their own and other people's affairs, but unlike religion it does not concern itself with ultimate questions of meaning and existence.

  5 The sociology of religion does not ask whether religion is 'true'.

> Durkheimians see religion as 'binding' society together.

> Weberians see religion as dealing with the problem of 'theodicy' – the search for meaning.

2 Psychological approaches to religion

- Sigmund Freud (1856–1939): When individuals are faced with **limit-situations** (such as extreme pain or fear of death) they relapse into infantile responses of what they would like to happen. In *Totem and Taboo* (1913) Freud put forward the view that 'wish-fulfilment is a prominent factor in religious motivation.'

- In *The Future of an Illusion* (1927) Freud declared that 'God is nothing other than an exalted father.' According to his theory of the Oedipus Complex the son is jealous of his father's relationship with his mother, and unconsciously desires to kill his father and possess his mother. The son represses his hostility to his father, idealises him, and makes him into a God-figure.

- Bronislaw Malinowski (1884–1942) carried out anthropological research in the Trobriand Islands in the Pacific. He saw religion as helping people deal with life crises (such as death) which are potential threats to social cohesion. Malinowski observed that when islanders fished in the calm waters of the lagoon they did not use any religious rituals, but when faced with the dangers of fishing in the open sea beyond the barrier reef religious rituals were always used.

> The writer Brendan Behan alluded to 'limit-situations' when he said he was a 'daylight atheist'!

3 | Sociological approaches to religion

Examiners will expect you to be familiar with Durkheim's distinction between the sacred and the profane.

- Auguste Comte (1798–1857) saw the development of both the mind and society as passing through three distinct stages.

  1 theological: events are explained in terms of religion and magic;

  2 metaphysical: superstition declines and events are explained in terms of abstract concepts;

  3 positive: events are explained in purely scientific terms. Comte was convinced that religion would be replaced by science.

- Emile Durkheim saw 'the distinctive trait' of religious thought as the contrast between the sacred and the profane, between the holy and the secular. The central focus of religion is on the sacred – values which evoke attitudes of great respect and awe. In *The Elementary Forms of the Religious Life* (1912) Durkheim defined religion as 'beliefs and practices which relate to sacred things, that is to say, things set apart and forbidden.' Studies of Australian aborigine society showed that each tribe had its own **totem**. This is a natural object (such as a plant or animal) which serves as an emblem of the clan. The totem represents both the sacred and the social, it is 'at once the symbol of god and of society...'

- For Durkheim a key function of religion is to strengthen social cohesion and affirm the moral superiority of society over the individual. Joining together in communal religious activity promotes social solidarity. During religious ceremonies people feel overpowered by a force greater than themselves, a force which is a product of the collective ferment generated by the worshippers. Durkheim saw the worship of God as the disguised worship of society.

- In Durkheim's view religion is essential in *all* societies. He wrote (1912): 'There can be no society which does not feel the need of upholding and reaffirming at regular intervals the collective sentiments and collective ideas which make its unity and its personality.'

Perhaps today television and sport are the 'opium of the people'!

- Robert Bocock's *Ritual in Industrial Society* (1974) sees rituals as performing a number of vital pattern-maintenance functions. Ritual occasions heighten awareness of the obligations individuals have to society, reinforce cultural values, and engender a sense of belonging. But not all rituals are 'religious'. Sporting occasions, artistic events, and political meetings are examples of 'civic rituals'. Rituals are essential in all societies, but they do not have to be of a religious character.

- Marx said that 'Man makes religion, religion does not make man...Religion is the sigh of the oppressed creature, the heart of a heartless world...It is the opium of the people', *Economic and Philosophic Manuscripts of 1844*. Marx saw religion as a product of alienation and exploitation. The masses accept the miseries of this world in the illusory hope that those who suffer will be rewarded in the next. Religion provides a psychological compensation for distress and discourages people from seeking a political solution to their problems. It is a method of social control used by the dominant class to persuade people to accept their lot in life.

- Weber examined the relationship between social position and propensity to support different types of religion. The way of life of particular social groups makes them 'idea prone' – receptive to certain belief systems. Lower income groups (unlike higher income groups) are susceptible to the appeal of salvatiary and evangelical style religions.

4 | Religious organisations and movements

- **Church:** Churches are viewed as 'socially acceptable' by the majority of people. They have a predominantly inherited membership, are inclusive, and are restrained in their services. Churches tend to accept the established order, and require only a partial commitment from their members.

The Church–Sect Cycle is a key sociological concept.

- **Sects:** defined by Ernst Troeltsch (1865–1923) as 'small groups which aspire after inward perfection and aim at direct personal fellowship between the members.' Sects are religious protest groups. They have a converted membership, are exclusive, and their services are highly emotional. They tend to reject the established social order, and require a wholehearted commitment from their members. Religious status is substituted for social status.

- **Church–Sect Cycle Theory:** the compromises a church makes with the wider society lead some of its members to feel that it is no longer faithful to its original principles. Dissenting members break away and form a new religious group – a sect. The meetings of the sect attract recruits from economically deprived members of the church. They are highly emotional and stress the moral superiority of the poor. Over time the sect changes, meetings become more emotionally restrained, and sect members become more prosperous. The sect begins to take on the church-like characteristics it originally denounced. This leads to some of the less prosperous members to break away and form another sect. The whole cycle is then repeated once again.

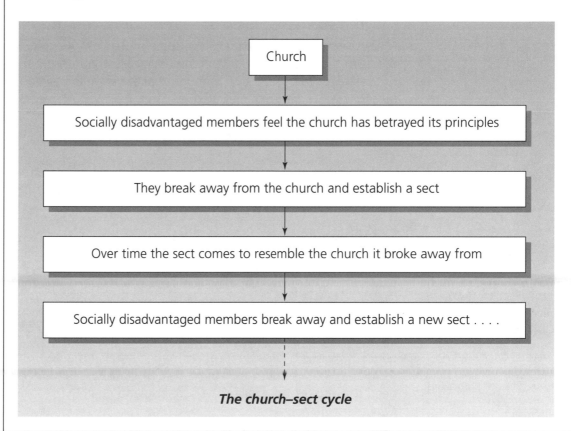

The church–sect cycle

- **Denominations:** with the passing of time sects become less opposed to prevailing societal values. Nonconformist groups like the Methodists began as sects and became denominations. They remain separate from the state (unlike churches) and do not reject the wider society (unlike sects). They occupy a mid-way position between churches and sects.

- **Cults:** are difficult to distinguish from sects. Many are short-lived, are based around a charismatic leader, have secretive beliefs, and tend to recruit marginal individuals. Factors leading to the growth in cults and sects include rapid social change, economic disadvantage, and individuals' search for meaning. Members are usually permitted to maintain other religious affiliations. The word 'cult' has a deviant image (partly because of the many tragic deaths associated with cults in recent years).

- **New religious movements** (NRMs) consist of two main types:

1 Religions which have emerged in Third World societies as a result of interactions

between indigenous religions and the religions of colonial settlers (such as Christianity). An example is the **cargo cults** which were widespread in the South Pacific between 1900 and 1950. Islanders observed that planes and ships brought consumer goods to the islands. Imitation airstrips and harbours were then constructed. All material goods were seen as having supernatural origins and it was widely believed that planes and ships would soon arrive with 'cargo' for the local inhabitants rather than for the western colonialists, Peter Worsley, *The Trumpet Shall Sound* (1968).

2 New religions have emerged in western industrial societies. The terms 'sect' and 'cult' are increasingly seen as unsatisfactory. Roy Wallis has classified religious groups according to their orientation to the world. **World-affirming NRMs** accept the values of society and offer their members the prospect of 'better jobs, higher IQ, greater success in personal relationships, etc.' (e.g. transcendental meditation). **World-accommodating NRMs** 'neither fully accept the norms and values of the surrounding society, nor entirely reject them by separating themselves off completely in communities of the like-minded' (e.g. Neo-Pentecostalism and Charismatic Renewal). **World-rejecting NRMs** are hostile to the values of society and require their members to withdraw from the secular world and lead a life based on their own distinctive principles (e.g. the 'Moonies' and the Hare Krishna movement).

- **Millenarian movements:** a classic study of religious movements in Western Europe between the 11th and 16th centuries was carried out by Norman Cohn, *The Pursuit of the Millennium*, (1970). This found that salvationary religious movements were most likely to emerge during times of famine or war. Members of these movements were drawn mainly from the ranks of the 'dispossessed poor' and were convinced that a miraculous transformation of daily life was about to occur.

5 | Key concepts

5.1 Religion as a social construction

- Religion is constructed by individuals in order to give a sense of purpose to their lives and create a 'universe of meaning.' Religion provides people with answers to ultimate questions and conveys a sense of living in 'a sacred cosmos.' (This phenomenological perspective is developed by Peter Berger, *The Sacred Canopy: Elements of a Sociological Theory of Religion* (1990).) In the view of Daniel Bell individuals create religious meaning because it meets fundamental and enduring emotional needs: 'religion is a constitutive part of man's consciousness (and meets) ... the existential need to confront the finalities of suffering and death', *The Cultural Contradictions of Capitalism* (1976).

5.2 Pluralisation of life-worlds

- In pre-industrial societies people inhabit a single 'life-world'. Religion provides a fixed universe of meaning, a single over-arching set of core beliefs. In industrial societies individuals experience a number of different 'life-worlds'. The values and ideas they encounter in the workplace may be quite different from those they encounter in the family. The mass media expose individuals to a plurality of beliefs and ideologies. The result is a collapse of certainties. The single universe of meaning provided by religion loses its plausibility, and secularisation (the decline of religion) is accelerated, P. Berger, B. Berger, and H. Kellner, *The Homeless Mind: Modernisation and Consciousness* (1974). (This concept can be linked to the post-modernist view that total explanations of the purpose of history, metanarratives, have lost their plausibility.)

5.3 Internal secularisation

- In the USA over 40% of the adult population attend a religious service every week. However, in the view of Will Herberg, American churches do not provide 'authentic religion': going to church in the USA is a way of expressing commitment to the local community and integrating into the mainstream. The emphasis on services is on 'ethical behaviour and a good life' rather than theology and doctrine. Despite its packed churches America is a secular society, *Protestant, Catholic, Jew* (1960).

5.4 Social differentiation and societalisation

- 'Social differentiation is the set of processes by which specialised roles and institutions concerned with very specific functions develop; for example, institutions to handle education, health and welfare, all of which were once the concern of the church.

- Societalisation refers to the process by which more and more aspects of life come under the influence of broad levels of social organisation such as the state and are decreasingly matters for the local community... As this community becomes less significant in the impersonal conditions of modern life religion loses its significance', Malcolm Harrison, 'Secularisation', *Sociology Review*, April 1998.

6 | The debate on secularisation

The Latin *saeculum* means 'this age'. A **secular society** is one concerned with the affairs of this age, not the sacred. **Secularisation** refers to the process whereby religious thinking, practices and institutions are in decline and lose their social significance.

6.1 Evidence put forward by supporters of the secularisation thesis

- Church attendance has continued to decline. It is estimated that between 1860 and 1910 over a quarter of the adult population in Britain were active church members. The report 'Faith in the City' (1985) found that less than 1.5% of the population attended a Church of England service on an average Sunday (0.85% in inner city areas). In 1996 less than one-third of the 4.5 million Catholics in England and Wales went to church on an average Sunday.

- Church membership has declined. Churches have different definitions of 'membership' but, on their own criteria, membership numbers have generally fallen (e.g. since 1950 the number of Methodists has fallen from almost 750,000 to under 450,000).

- Survey research reveals a decline in the proportion of the population in Britain who believe in life after death – from 54% in 1957 to 27% in 1991. Over the same period the proportion who believed in the Devil fell from 34% to 24%.

- In 1901 only 15% of all marriages were conducted in registry offices. In 1997 over half of the 324,000 marriages which took place in Britain were civil services. The only religious ceremony that has not declined significantly is that conducted during burials.

- The political power of the Church of England and its influence on the law has declined. Sunday shopping has now been legalised, whereas in 1854 religious pressure led to public houses being closed on Sundays, and in 1855 to the sale of newspapers and tobacco being forbidden.

- The Churches have themselves been secularised. Leading clergymen have publicly challenged such traditional doctrines as the Virgin Birth and the Resurrection.

- There has been a marked increase in the prestige of scientific as against religious explanations of events. Natural calamities are no longer explained in terms of divine punishment from God.

> Examiners will expect you to give a clear definition of secularisation.

> In deciding whether or not religion is in decline you must decide how 'religion' is to be defined.

Those who support
the Secularisation
Thesis point to the
decline in church
attendance.

- Sects and cults are 'last refuges' for those who believe in the supernatural. Only by cutting themselves off from the wider society is it possible for their members to retain their religious beliefs. They tend to attract drop-outs and contribute little to society's moral values.

6.2 Evidence put forward by critics of the secularisation thesis

- Although attendance at Christian churches has declined there has been an increase in attendance of new religious groups. The Church–Sect Cycle theory reminds us that for every church in decline a new sect will be gaining fresh converts. Immigration has revitalised some religions, and there are now twice as many Muslims in Britain as Methodists.

Those who oppose
the Secularisation
Thesis point to the
growth in new
religious
movements.

- The decline in membership of Christian churches has to be looked at from a phenomenological perspective (i.e. in terms of the subjective experience of individuals – what religion *means* to the participants). The high church-attendance rates of the Victorian era partly reflected a quest for middle-class respectability. In some rural areas individuals were fined for not attending church.

- The 'myth of a religious past' has come under increasing challenge. Historians have noted that in urban working-class areas in the 19th century church attendance was always a minority activity.

- Survey research reveals that only 10% of the population in Britain do not believe in God, M. Hamilton, Secularisation, *Sociology Review*, April 1998.

- Religion continues to be linked with important social institutions. The Queen is Head of the Church of England, 26 Bishops sit in the House of Lords, the Charter of the BBC requires it to transmit religious programmes, prayers are said in Parliament, etc.

- David Martin argues that the popularity of 'subterranean theologies' (such as astrology, the occult, and psychic phenomena) is evidence of a widespread religious consciousness in society, *The Religious and the Secular* (1969).

- Religion has not declined but has simply changed its form of expression. It has undergone a process of **individuation** whereby instead of accepting imposed religious doctrines individuals now search for and construct their own ultimate meanings. The central focus of religion has shifted from collective worship to an individual quest for meaning, Robert Bellah, *New Religious Consciousness and the Crisis of Modernity* (1976).

7 | Religion and social change

- Durkheim and Marx saw religion as a set of beliefs and practices which act as a brake on social change. Both functionalists and Marxists view religion as a mechanism of social control contributing to social stability and the preservation of the status quo. Religion is portrayed as a conservative force which works to keep the existing structure of society intact.

- In *The Protestant Ethic and the Spirit of Capitalism* (1904–5) Max Weber put forward the view that religion can act as a force for social change: ideas can change the course of history.

Weber's book
The Protestant
Ethic is one of
the classic studies
in sociological
literature.

- In Weber's view the development of capitalism depended above all on the **rationalism** of western culture. The 'spirit of modern capitalism' centres on the rational and systematic pursuit of profit. Both ascetic Protestantism (ascetic meaning 'beliefs practised with a high degree of rigour and self-denial') and capitalist enterprise seek to subject everyday life to active self control and systematisation.

- The central idea in Protestantism was the notion that individuals come nearer to God by fulfilling their vocation or 'business in life'. Unlike Catholicism, Puritanism completely eliminated the Church and the sacraments from the attainment of salvation. The individual looked to his own work and life for signs that he was one of the elect, one of the pre-destined few chosen by God. Calvinists believed that God had already decided who was predestined 'into everlasting life' and who was predestined 'to everlasting death'.

- Wasting time was regarded as sinful. According to John Wesley, Christians should 'gain all they can, save all they can – grow rich.' Benjamin Franklin warned that he who 'spends a groat a day idly, spends idly over £6 a year, which is the price for the use of £100.' All enjoyment of possessions, all luxurious consumption, was sinful. All thrift, effort, and hard work was the fulfilment of the 'call of God'.

- Weber described Protestantism as standing 'at the cradle of modern economic man.' In its Calvinist form it constituted the 'seedbed of the capitalistic economy'.

- Supporters of Weber point out that in Japan (the only Asian country to independently embark on capitalist development) there are striking similarities between Protestantism and some Japanese religions. Ideas can act as a catalyst for social change.

- Weber did not put forward a monocausal theory of change (i.e. one single factor – ideas – can change history). In his view social change was the result of ideas *and* economic factors interacting with each other.

- Historians have pointed to flaws in Weber's analysis. For example, capitalism had developed in some parts of Europe before Protestantism emerged as a major force.

You must know your 'monocausal' from your 'multicausal'!

8 | Checklist of key terms and concepts

The Sacred and the Profane   Monotheistic   Polytheistic   Church   Sect   Denomination Cult   Church–Sect   Cycle Theory   Cargo cult   Totem   Millenarian movement   Secular society   Pluralisation of life-worlds   Internal secularisation   Individuation   New religious movements   World-affirming   World-accommodating   World-rejecting   Monocausal theory of change

9 | Further reading

Bruce, S. (1995) *Religion in Modern Britain*, London, Oxford University Press.

Morgan, I. (15.10.93) 'God in the Twilight Zone', *Times Educational Supplement*.

Thompson, I. (1986) *Religion*, London, Longman.

Wallis, R. (1984) *Elementary Forms of the New Religious Life*, London, Routledge.

Power and politics

1 | Definition of Politics

- The word politics (from the Greek *polis*) refers to a community of citizens who belong to a city-state.

- **Politics 1** is the study of power and conflict: 'the exercise of constraint in any relationship is political.'

- **Politics 2** is the study of the state, political institutions and government, Peter Worsley, *Introducing Sociology* (1977).

2 | Power, influence and authority

Bertrand Russell believed that power is the fundamental concept in social science, just as energy is the fundamental concept in physics.

- Thomas Hobbes saw human beings as power seekers. In *Leviathan* (1651) he referred to 'a general inclination of all mankind, a perpetual and restless desire of power after power, that ceaseth only in death.'

- Friedrich Nietzsche (1844–1900) said 'This world is the will to power and nothing else besides', *The Will To Power* (1888).

- Bertrand Russell defined power as 'the production of intended effects.'

- Max Weber defined power as 'the probability that one actor within a social relationship will be in a position to carry out his will, even against resistance.'

- C. Wright Mills defined the powerful as 'those who are able to realise their will, even if others resist it.'

- *Coercive power* is the ability of X to get Y to act in conformity with his intentions by making things unpleasant for Y if he does not comply.

- *Inducive power* is the ability of X to get Y to act in conformity with his intentions by providing something attractive for Y in order to gain his compliance.

- Talcott Parsons defined influence as 'a way of having an effect on the attitudes and opinions of others through intentional action.' Influence consists of the capacity to convince, to persuade, to change the attitudes and opinions of other people.

Examiners will expect you to clearly distinguish power from authority.

- Max Weber defined authority as the 'probability that a *command* will be obeyed.' Authority is legitimate power. People consent to obey because they believe in the legitimacy of those who rule. (However consent may be the product of manipulation – of individuals having their beliefs shaped by others.) Illegitimate power depends on the threat of force and coercion.

- Hannah Arendt noted that 'the greatest enemy of authority is contempt.'

3 | The nature of power

3.1 Three faces of power

- Stephen Lukes sees power as having three dimensions, *Power: A Radical View* (1974).

  1 **Success in decision making** (e.g. a powerful group wants parliament to pass a particular law. The group gets its way, the law is passed, even in the face of opposition from other groups).

2 **Fixing the agenda** (e.g. a powerful group wants to stop an issue from being publicly debated. It gets its way and the issue is not even discussed – it is made a 'non-decision').

3 **Mobilising bias** (e.g. a powerful group wants to veto a particular policy, although most people stand to benefit from this policy. The powerful group then manipulates public opinion and succeeds in persuading most people that they should oppose a policy which would benefit them).

- Note: Weber has been criticised for being a 'methodological individualist' and defining power in terms of one individual being able to impose his / her will on another. But power also has a collective dimension (e.g. the mobilisation of bias cannot be effected by the will of a single individual).

Fixing the agenda and mobilising bias are examples of the hidden dimension of power.

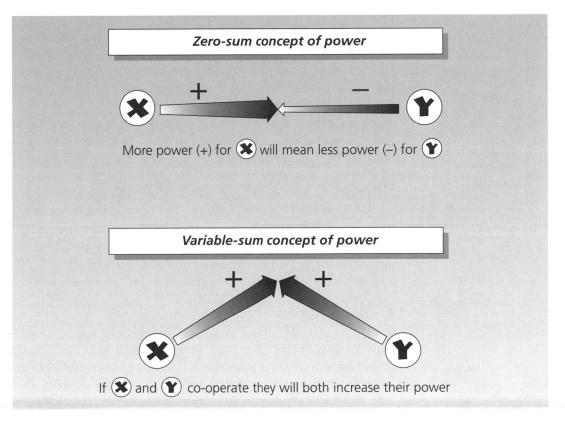

3.2 Zero-sum and variable-sum concepts of power

Marxists and Functionalists will define power in different ways.

- Conflict theorists see power in **zero-sum terms**: the amount of power is fixed, and the more power 'X' has the less power 'Y' has.

- Consensus theorists see power in **variable-sum terms**: the amount of power is not fixed but can be decreased or increased, and the more X and Y work together the more power there will be for both of them.

3.3 The increase in the 'power of power'

- During this century the organisational effectiveness of the state has increased dramatically – the 'power of power' (in Giovanni Sartori's phrase) has grown.

- According to C. Wright Mills, power in the USA has been concentrated in the hands of the top military, political, and economic leaders. 'As the circle of those who decide is narrowed, as the means of decision are centralised and the consequences of decisions becomes enormous, then the course of great events rests upon the decisions of determinable circles', *The Power Élite* (1956).

- Michael Mann refers to the four key sources of power as economic, political, military, and ideological, *The Sources of Social Power* (1993).

3.4 Instrumentalist and structuralist theories of state power

Miliband versus Poulantzas was a classic debate in political sociology.

- In the view of Ralph Miliband the economically dominant class exercises a decisive degree of political power. Key state institutions such as the higher civil service, the military, and the judiciary are staffed by individuals from an upper-class background (public schools and Oxbridge) who use the state as an instrument of class rule, *The State In Capitalist Society* (1973).

- In the view of Nicos Poulantzas it is a mistake to see the state as being used by individuals. It is the state which uses individuals. The function of the state is to serve the long-term interests of capital, and these may be in conflict with the short-term interests of particular sections of the capitalist class. Consequently the state must possess a degree of relative autonomy. *Classes in Contemporary Capitalism* (1975).

3.5 The micro-physics of power

Foucault is now regarded as a key sociological theorist.

- Michel Foucault (1926–84) sees the presence of power, domination, and resistance in all social processes including 'discourses' – language, knowledge, and all forms of communication. Foucault shows how, from the late 18th century on, asylums were built to house individuals defined as 'mad', *Madness and Civilisation: A History of Insanity in the Age of Reason* (1961). In *Discipline and Punish: The Birth of the Prison* (1975) Foucault refers to the Panopticon prison structure designed by Jeremy Bentham. This enabled large numbers of prisoners to be kept under surveillance by a small number of (unseen) guards. For Foucault the Panopticon is a metaphor for life in modern society: surveillance and control are everywhere, from the CCTV in the town centre to the telephone being tapped, to data on our credit rating. The struggle for power is felt in every crevice of existence.

3.6 Globalisation

The debate on whether globalisation has significantly reduced the power of the state is a major debate in contemporary sociology.

- This consists of the 'growing interdependence between different peoples, regions and countries in the world', Anthony Giddens, *Sociology* (1997). Global trade and communications have brought about a 'shrinkage' in time and space. Globalisation has also been accompanied by the emergence of the **risk society**. New threats to the survival of both individuals and the human species – **manufactured risks** – have been created, including threats created by the human species itself (e.g. polluting the air, the seas, and the earth).

- According to S. Lash and J. Urry a system of 'disorganised capitalism' is coming into existence, *The End of Organised Capitalism* (1987). Transnational corporations have drained power away from governments. The decline in the role of the nation state and the break-up and fragmentation of the established system of international relations has been described by some theorists as **neo-medievalism**.

- P. Hirst and G. Thompson reject the view that the state is being 'hollowed out' and depleted of power. Nation states retain a monopoly of the legitimate use of force in their territories, still hold considerable economic and political power, and continue to be a focal point of cultural identity. The globalisation of the world economy has been much exaggerated, *Globalization In Question* (1996).

4 Theories of the distribution of power

4.1 Pluralist view

- Montesquieu (who wrote *The Spirit of the Laws* (1748)) has considerable influence on modern theories of pluralism. In France the three key institutions of power – the executive, legislature, and judiciary – were in the hands of one person – the monarch. However, in Britain a '**separation of powers**' existed: government, parliament, and the courts were controlled by different people who constantly checked and limited each others' power. Liberty is 'power cut into pieces.' The American Constitution was based on the concept of separation of powers.

- Classical pluralists like Robert Dahl claim there is no single centre of power which imposes its will on other institutions. In *Who Governs?* (1961) Dahl studied decision-making in the Eastern USA city of New Haven and concluded that no one group regularly succeeded in getting its own way. In fact, the most striking feature of New Haven politics was the 'extent to which it is specialised, with individuals who are influential in one sector tending not to be influential in another.' The USA is a **polyarchal democracy** – the many (poly) rule (archo).

- Suzanne Keller is a multiple-élite theorist who argues that no single group in industrial society can have absolute power, *Beyond the Ruling Class: Strategic Élites in Modern Society* (1968). In pre-industrial societies it was possible for a single élite to organise all the leadership functions needed to keep society afloat. But modern society is far too complex for this to be possible. Consequently power is shared out amongst those élites which possess the specialised professional skills required to run an industrial society: political, economic, military, scientific, moral, and cultural.

- **Key themes of classical pluralism:** society is 'open' and made up of many interests. Individuals have 'cross-cutting ties' – they support 'Group X' on one issue and 'Group Y' on another. No one interest or élite group is dominant. Business élites face the 'counter-vailing power' of the state and trade unions. Skill and organisation can be as politically effective as money and wealth. Ordinary individuals can influence government through elections, political parties, and pressure groups. Even apathetic citizens exert an indirect influence since politicians need to anticipate their wishes in order to win elections. (**The Law of Anticipated Reactions**).

- **Criticisms of classical pluralism:** it ignores the bias of the state towards well-organised and wealthy pressure groups. Business is a dominant influence on government. The influence of ordinary citizens on decision-making is exaggerated. Some groups (such as the poor and the unemployed) can be ignored by government.

- These criticisms led writers like Dahl to modify their position and formulate what has become known as élite pluralism. This acknowledges that some groups have greater influence on decision-making than others, and that the interests of socially and economically disadvantaged groups are under-represented.

4.2 Marxist view

- The state is not (as pluralists claim) a neutral umpire, but is biased towards the propertied classes. Top industrialists are automatically given '**insider status**' and represented on Whitehall committees.

- Business élites have a major say in government decision-making. The dramatic inequalities which exist in the distribution of wealth and income are a reflection of their hold on power.

- The powerful 'set the agenda' of political debate. Pluralists ignore the hidden dimension of power: élite groups can prevent some issues from being publicly debated. Some individuals will not even attempt to say certain things because they know in advance that their views will not be accepted by those in power.

- The needs and interests of the bottom fifth of the population are ignored. The 'law of anticipated reactions' only applies to well-heeled sections of the electorate.

- Critics of the Marxist view claim it exaggerates the power of business, ignores divisions amongst economic élites, and underestimates the **'counter-vailing' power** that can be exerted by ordinary people in a democratic society. Wealth is unequally concentrated in Britain, but economic power does not guarantee political power.

The law of anticipated reactions is an important concept in political sociology.

Is the state a biased or neutral umpire? This is a key issue in the debate between Pluralists and their critics.

4.3 Élitest view

- **Vilfredo Pareto** (1848–1923): explained politics in terms of enduring psychological characteristics. All societies are divided between the mass of the population – the non-élite – and the élite. The élite consists of two sections – the non-governing élite, and the governing élite ('a smaller, choicer class that effectively exercises control'). The two main types of élite are the tough-minded '**Lions**' (who rely on brute force and cunning), and the tender-minded '**Foxes**' (who rely on cunning and intelligence). 'Lion' élites are overthrown because they use too much force, 'Fox' élites because they use too little. History is 'a graveyard of aristocracies'.

- **Gaetano Mosca** (1858–1941): élite rule is inevitable because of:

  1 Organisation: the élite is quantitatively a minority, but because of its superior capacity for organisation is qualitatively a majority. The '**three Cs**' (consciousness, cohesion, and conspiracy) come naturally to the élite.

  2 Ideology: every ruling élite has to find a justification for its power – or a 'political formula' as Mosca put it. ('Every tyrant must sleep' as Thomas Hobbes put it.) Elections are simply the process whereby a member of the élite 'has himself elected by the voters'.

- **Robert Michels** (1876–1936): wrote the classic study *Political Parties. A Sociological Study of the Oligarchical Tendencies of Modern Democracy* (1911). The study was partly based on Michels' experiences in the German Social Democratic Party (SPD). Michels believed there was an **Iron Law of Oligarchy** – once organisation reaches a certain size power is concentrated in the hands of the few at the top. Participatory democracy and large-scale organisation are incompatible because a large organisation needs a full-time leadership. The leaders acquire technical skills, political know-how, and control over finance and internal communications. In a political party or trade union a worker who becomes a full-time official experiences a rise in social status and becomes 'bourgeoisified'. Psychological forces are also at work. The masses are prone to deference which enables the 'natural greed for power' of the oligarchs to thrive unmolested.

- **C. Wright Mills** (1916–62): in *The Power Élite* (1956) Mills saw power in the USA as divided into three levels: 1. the masses: essentially powerless and manipulated into passive conformity by the mass media. 2. the middle range of power: a key institution is Congress (the US Parliament). It has limited power and is mainly concerned with issues of public expenditure and taxation. 3. the Power Élite: composed of top political, economic, and military leaders, it takes decisions of at least national consequence (e.g. dropping the atomic bomb on Japan and military intervention in Korea).

5 | The Establishment

- Henry Fairlie (*The Spectator*, September 1955) provided the first definition of the Establishment. 'The exercise of power in Britain (more specifically in England) cannot be understood unless it is recognised that it is exercised socially...the "Establishment" can be seen at work in the activities, not only of the Prime Minister, the Archbishop of Canterbury and the Earl Marshal, but also of such lesser mortals as the chairman of the Arts Council, the Director-General of the BBC, and even the editor of *The Times Literary Supplement*...'.

- Anthony Sampson, *Anatomy of Britain* (1962): 'The rulers are not at all close-knit or united ... they are not a single Establishment but a ring of Establishments, with slender connections. The frictions and balances between the different circles are the supreme safeguard of democracy. No one man can stand in the centre, for there is no centre.'

- Jean Blondel, *Voters, Parties and Leaders. The Social Fabric of British Politics* (1965): members of the Establishment possess attitudes which 'make them "acceptable" to other members of the ruling group. The theory (of the Establishment) is based on the

---

The Iron Law of Oligarchy is a classic theory in political sociology.

Examiners will expect you to be familiar with Mills' concept of The Power Elite.

Note the distinctions between power bloc, power élite, establishment and ruling class.

idea of a certain social network, which has its manners, its values, its readily accepted *savoir faire ...*' Membership of a power élite, in contrast, does not require individuals to have 'the right background or the right accent'.

- Martin Jacques, 'The Establishment. It's Back', *Sunday Times* (17.1.93): society has become less cohesive and more individualistic. At the top are the privileged 10%, at the bottom the 30% who are dispossessed, with the broad middle mass in between. However, the power of the Establishment has not changed. A survey of the backgrounds of the people who occupied 100 of the top jobs in 1992 (in banks, big companies, the army, the Foreign Office, and the BBC) found that 54% had attended Oxbridge, 66% had attended public schools, and 96% were men.

- John Scott, *Who Rules Britain?* (1991): the Establishment forms part of a **power bloc**. 'A power bloc is an informal coalition of social groups, often under the leadership of one group, which actually holds the levers of political power in society...British society in the twentieth century has been ruled by just such a power bloc, headed by the upper-class members of the 'establishment'... Britain has an upper class that dominates government, but it does not have a ruling class.'

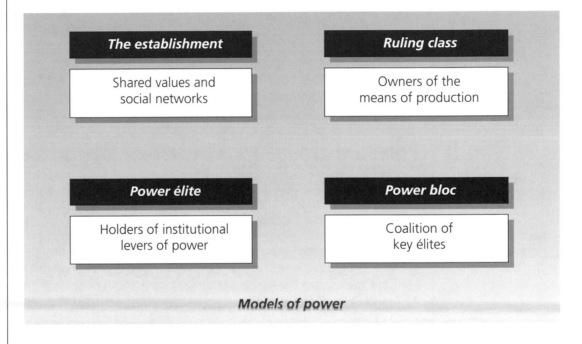

Models of power

6 | Power in totalitarian states

Examiners will expect you to be able to define Totalitarianism.

'**Totalitarian**' means comprehensive or all embracing. It refers to a population brought under the total control of its rulers. The term was first used by Mussolini in 1925. Leonard Schapiro defines totalitarianism as 'a new form of dictatorship which grew up after the First World War. It was characterised by the predominance of the leader of the victorious movement who aimed at total control over state, society, and the individual', *Totalitarianism* (1972).

- C. Friedrich and Z. Brzezinski set out 6 factors which are common to all totalitarian societies: 1. an official ideology or set of beliefs to which everyone is supposed to adhere; 2. a single mass party, usually led by one man; 3. a monopoly of control of all military weapons; 4. central control of the economy; 5. a monopoly of mass communications; 6. a system of terroristic police control.

- An authoritarian dictatorship ignores public opinion and disregards individual rights. A totalitarian dictatorship uses modern technology to maximise domination and mobilise the entire population in support of its ideology. Every aspect of social existence – private and public – is controlled by the state.

7 | Power in communist states

- **The theory of the new class.** This was put forward by Milovan Djilas, *The New Class: an Analysis of the Communist System* (1957) – 'the communist revolution, conducted in the name of doing away with classes, has resulted in the most complete authority of any single new class.' He defined the new class as being composed of those who have 'special privileges and economic preference because of the administrative monopoly they hold.'

- **The key to the power of the new class is not ownership but control.** The political bureaucracy controls the state, exploits the working class, acquires privileges, and passes these on (via 'connections' rather than the inheritance of property) to its children. Communist states are not 'half-way houses' between capitalist inequality and workers' democracy but simply a new form of exploitation. The power exercised by higher party officials is greater than that wielded by political élites in capitalist states.

- **The theory of the degenerate workers' state.** This was put forward by Leon Trotsky, *The Revolution Betrayed: the Soviet Union, what it is and where it is going* (1936). Trotsky believed the Soviet Union was 'a contradictory society, halfway between capitalism and socialism.' The state-owned economy made it a 'proletarian' society. But because the Soviet working class had hardly emerged from 'destitution and darkness' a new ruling group – the bureaucracy – was able to take power. The bureaucracy was not a class since it had 'neither stocks nor bonds.' But it was a 'privileged and commanding stratum' which exploited the rest of the population.

> The revolutions of 1989 led to the collapse of most communist states. But China, Cuba and Vietnam are still officially described as communist.

8 | Pressure groups

- **Unlike political parties, pressure groups do not seek to capture political office.** They attempt to influence government policy but do not seek to become the government.

- **A classic theorist** who pioneered the study of pressure groups was Arthur Bentley, *The Process of Government* (1904). His theory was based on investigations of the Chicago City Council and the Illinois State legislature and he concluded that decision-making is shaped by powerful pressure groups (which often meet behind closed doors).

- **Protective (or *interest*) groups** aim to defend specific interests (e.g. companies, professional associations, trade unions).

- **Promotional (or *cause*) groups** are based on shared attitudes rather than sectional interests (e.g. Friends of the Earth, the League Against Cruel Sports, Age Concern).

- **Insider groups** (unlike **outsider groups**) are regularly listened to and consulted by government. Having insider status means a pressure group is represented on the advisory committees in Whitehall which influence policy. It belongs to a **policy community** – an established network of contacts with civil service departments and ministers.

- **Pressure group activity is not new.** In the 18th and 19th centuries protective groups (such as the East India Company) and promotional groups (such as the Anti-Corn Law League) were influential. The Labour Party was formed as a result of pressure group activity (i.e. the trade unions). The increase in government intervention in the economy, the growth in mass democracy, the establishment of the welfare state, and the expansion in education has increased the role of pressure groups.

- **In order to influence decision-making pressure groups focus their activities on:**

  1 The government and the civil service in London, and the institutions of the European Union in Brussels.

  2 Parliament and Members of Parliament.

  3 Public opinion.

> Examiners will expect you to be able to distinguish between insider and outsider groups.

- **A social movement** is 'a collective attempt to further a common interest or secure a common goal, through collective action outside the sphere of established institutions', Anthony Giddens, *Sociology* (1997). Social movements involve:

  1 at least occasional mass mobilisation;

  2 tendency towards loose organisational structure;

  3 spasmodic activity;

  4 working at least in part outside established institutional frameworks;

  5 bringing about change (or perhaps preserving aspects of the social order) as a central aim', Alan Scott, *Political Culture and Social Movements*, in J. Allen *et al.* (eds) – *Political and Economic Forms of Modernity* (1992).

- **New social movements (NSMs)** tend to be post-materialist (concerned with issues of identity and quality of life rather than defence of economic interests), based on informal networks, and draw their support mainly from the new middle class (e.g. the women's movement and the ecological movement). **Old social movements (OSMs)** tend to be concerned with issues of economic power, have more formal structures, and draw their support mainly from the working class (e.g. the labour movement and trade unions).

Examiners will expect you to know your OSMs from your NSMs!

8.1 The case for pressure groups

- Without pressure groups political parties would have a monopoly on political participation. Membership of parties has generally been in decline, and pressure groups provide an outlet for those who would otherwise not get involved in the democratic process.

- They perform a key '*interest articulation function*' conveying expert advice and information to the policy-making machine.

- They represent and defend the interests of minorities which might otherwise be ignored by government and political parties.

- They contribute to political education raising public awareness of issues and educating their own members through involvement in democratic politics.

- They help create an open society by increasing dialogue between government and the governed.

8.2 The case against pressure groups

Are you a Burkean?

- They are unrepresentative and are led by activists who do not reflect the feelings of their members – in the view of S.E. Finer 'little better than cranks and bores', *Anonymous Empire* (1968).

- Protective pressure groups exert influence secretively behind closed doors. This conflicts with the Burkean concept of democracy whereby issues are debated and decided by MPs. (Edmund Burke (1729–97) argued that an MP should be a representative and not a delegate of his constituents.)

Examiners will expect you to formulate your own position on the desirability of pressure groups influencing government policy.

- They are selfishly concerned with furthering their narrow sectional interests at the expense of the public interest.

- The most successful pressure groups are those which are wealthy and well organised. Producer interests override consumer interests, and weaker groups are left out in the cold.

- Pressure groups '*over-load*' the state. Governments either appease the demands of pressure groups by increasing public spending which results in economic decline, or they resist them which can lead to a 'legitimation crisis' and a collapse in public confidence in the political system.

9 | Political participation

- This is 'the voluntary activity of an individual in political affairs, including ... voting; membership and activity connected with political groups such as interest groups, political movements and parties; office holding in political institutions; the exercise of political leadership; informal activities such as taking part in political discussions, or attendance at political events such as demonstrations; attempts to persuade the authorities or members of the public to act in particular ways in relation to political goals', G. Roberts and A. Edwards, *A New Dictionary of Political Analysis* (1991).

- Only a minority of the population take an active interest in politics. In Britain between 10 and 15% report being 'keenly interested' in politics. Some 26% take no part in politics (not even voting), while 1.5% are 'complete activists' G. Parry *et al.* – *Participation and Democracy: Political Activity and Attitudes in Contemporary Britain* (1989). In the USA the Survey Research Centre at the University of Michigan found that 7% of the population participated in politics; 20% were opinion leaders (they initiated discussion in day-to-day relationships); and 20% were apathetic (unaware of political issues).

- Levels of political literacy are low. Only one in four American citizens are aware that the Chinese Government is communist. 81% were unable to name the three branches of government (executive, legislature, and judiciary). In Britain only 30% of the public are able to name three government ministers. 42% do not know that Britain possesses nuclear weapons.

- Political partisanship is of a low intensity. The classic study by G. Almond and S. Verba, *The Civic Culture: Political Attitudes and Democracy in Five Nations* (1963) found that in both the UK and the USA 90% of respondents said it would make no difference if their child married a supporter of another political party.

- A key influence on participation is socio-economic status. Higher-status individuals are more likely to vote and to hold elective office. Lower-status individuals tend to be less confident about engaging in politics.

- Social factors influence participation. Those in rural areas are less likely to be politically active than those in urban areas (with the exception of inner city areas). Participation rates increase with length of residence in a particular location. Men are more likely to be politically active than women. Young unmarried individuals have the lowest levels of participation. In Britain electoral turn-out is lowest amongst members of the Afro-Caribbean community.

- Personality factors influence participation. Extroverted, sociable individuals are the most likely to be politically active. Studies of student activists have found that the majority come from professional middle-class families and scored high on extrovertism.

> Those who need to be the most politically active tend to be the least politically active!

10 | Voting behaviour and democracy

- Voting behaviour is sometimes referred to as **psephology**. The term is derived from the pebbles (*psepholos*) which were used to vote in ancient Athens.

- The word *democracy* comes from the Greek *demos* (people) and *kratos* (power), i.e. the people exercise power. Democracy was first developed in Athens in 4 BC. Athenian democracy was based on **direct democracy** – all citizens aged over 30 were able to debate public issues and pass laws in the General Assembly of Citizens. However, only between 20,000 and 40,000 of the 300,000 population of Athens were citizens. The majority were slaves. Democracy in the United Kingdom is based on **indirect or representative democracy** – representatives are elected to debate and pass laws on behalf of the rest of the population.

> Examiners will expect you to be familiar with the distinction between direct and indirect democracy.

10.1 Key concepts in voting behaviour

- **Tactical voting:** a voter supports a candidate who is not his/her first choice in order to prevent the election of the least-liked party. This has become increasingly important since 1979.

- **Partisan dealignment:** puts forward the claim that there has been a decline in the proportion of voters who are strongly attached to a political party.

- **Class dealignment:** puts forward the claim that compared with the 1950s and 1960s class has less influence on the way people vote. The alignment between class and voting is weakened (e.g. more middle-class people vote Labour and more working-class people vote Conservative).

- **Volatility:** changes in voting behaviour between successive elections. As voters' attachment to political parties weakens it becomes increasingly difficult to predict the results of elections.

- **Regional swings:** in the 1950s there was a uniform swing in constituencies throughout Britain. In recent elections there have been significant variations in voting patterns between different regions.

- **The incumbency effect:** an MP who has held a seat for a considerable time builds up a personal following (estimated at between 700 and 2,000 votes).

- **The Cube Rule:** the electoral system exaggerates the lead of the winning party when votes are converted into seats. (If votes are divided in the ratio of X:Y, the seats won will be in the ratio $X^3: Y^3$.) The electoral system worked to the advantage of the Labour Party in the 1997 election.

Partisan and Class Dealignment are key psephological concepts.

11 | Theories of voting behaviour

11.1 Family socialisation

- In the view of David Butler and Donald Stokes, *Political Change in Britain* (1974), party loyalties are acquired early in the childhood home. *Political socialisation* (the process whereby people acquire their attitudes to politics) means that family and class background are the crucial influences on voting, and once political allegiances have been formed they are likely to endure throughout an individual's lifetime.

- This theory is an example of an *expressive* model of voting: voting is viewed as a symbolic act which expresses individuals' allegiance to their social background.

- Critics see this theory as based on a static model of political socialisation. Butler and Stokes predicted that the Labour Party would become increasingly successful since a growing proportion of new voters would have been socialised into politics by Labour voting parents. Yet by 1983 Labour's share of the vote had slumped to 28.3%. R. Rose and I. McAllister have put forward a 'Lifetime Learning Model', *The Loyalties of Voters: A Lifetime Learning Model* (1990). They point out that factors other than family background (e.g. the performance of parties in government, and changes in party ideologies and policies) also have an influence on voting behaviour.

Examiners will expect you to be able to distinguish between expressive and instrumental models of voting.

11.2 Embourgeoisement

- This theory was put forward by Ferdinand Zweig in *The Worker in the Affluent Society* (1961). Rising living standards and increased prosperity lead workers to adopt middle-class (bourgeois) lifestyles. Owner-occupation, car ownership, package holidays, and possession of consumer durables change working-class consciousness.

- A 'new' working class has been formed which is more visible in the south of England than elsewhere. Its members are less likely to belong to a trade union and more likely

Examiners will expect you to be familiar with the concept of embourgeoisement – and to spell it correctly!

to own property, shares, personal pensions, and health insurance. It is composed of 'privatised instrumentalists' (i.e. individuals who are primarily concerned with improving their own economic situation). The trade union leader Ron Todd (general secretary of the TGWU) had this 'new' working class in mind when he declared that a well-paid dock worker 'with a little place in Marbella' was no longer responding to calls to free him from his misery.

- Embourgeoisement theorists predicted that support for the Labour Party would continue to decline (it peaked at 13.9 million in the 1951 General Election) and that an increasing proportion of manual workers would support the Conservative Party.

- Critics point out that a 'modernised' Labour Party (Wilson in 1964 and Blair in 1997) can win the support of affluent workers. In 1997 the Labour Party polled 13.5 million votes.

11.3 Rational choice voting

- This theory was first put forward by Anthony Downs, *An Economic Theory of Democracy* (1957). It is sometimes referred to as 'pocket-book' voting and it is an example of an **instrumental model of voting**: voting is seen as a means by which to maximise one's economic interests. (The 'what's in it for me?' syndrome.)

- Downs makes an analogy with consumerism. When a shopper chooses between goods on offer, s/he takes into account the manufacturer's reputation for quality of product. Thus the Conservative Party was successful in the 1980s because voters thought that the 'pay-off' from voting for Mrs Thatcher would be lower income tax, being able to buy their council house, obtaining shares in privatised industries, etc.

- Critics point out that if voters were selfishly 'rational' voters there would be little point in even making the effort of going to the polling station to cast a vote. Almost anything which increased an individual's sense of well-being will be more productive than walking to the polling station, e.g. going to a DIY store!

Instrumentalism is a key sociological concept.

11.4 Sectoral cleavages

- This concept was first put forward in the 1980s when Thatcherism was dominant, and is also known as the Radical Voting Model. Sectoral cleavages are divisions based on the split between those who rely on the public sector for consumption of services (such as transport and housing), and those who rely on the private sector. It also includes divisions between those who are employed in the public sector, and those who are employed in the private sector.

- Sectoral divisions have supplanted older class-based divisions. Those who rely on the public sector for employment and / or for substantial consumption provision are drawn towards support for 'statist' ideology (traditionally associated with the Labour Party). Those who work in the private sector and buy their key consumption requirements on the private market are drawn towards support for the 'anti-statist' / low taxation / low public expenditure policies traditionally associated with the Conservative Party.

- Critics point out that a significant numbers of voters have interests in both public and private sectors (e.g. the same individual may be employed in the private sector and have shares in private companies, but travel to work on public transport and have children who attend state schools).

Note the distinction between employment cleavages and consumption cleavages.

11.5 Labour voting as deviant voting

- In 'working-class Conservatism: a theory of political deviance', *British Journal of Sociology* 1967, Frank Parkin proposed that 'the values and symbols which have

historically attached to the Labour Party and other parties of the Left are in a sense deviant from those which emanate from the dominant institutional orders of this society.' (Examples of such institutions are the Established Church, the Monarchy, the ancient universities, etc.) To vote Labour is in a sense to be at odds with the dominant value system and is a 'symbolic act of deviance'.

- Such deviant voting will be most evident in areas where cultural 'barriers' insulate voters from the dominant values (e.g. in Welsh / Scottish / northern mining and engineering communities where trade unionism has been strong) and least evident in areas where working-class collectivist culture is weakest (e.g. in southern seaside resorts), i.e. the political culture of an area exerts a key influence on voting. Unless manual workers are 'protected' from the influence of the dominant institutions by their own counter-culture they will be 'pulled' towards voting for the Conservative Party.

- Critics point out that this theory is undermined by the changes in the ideology and policy agenda of 'New' (i.e. no longer 'deviant') General Labour. Since the 1997 Election it is possible to cross the country from east to west without passing through a single Conservative held constituency. In Blair's Britain a case could be made for describing a vote for the Conservative Party as a 'symbolic act of deviance'!

11.6 The Class Dealignment Model

- This theory has been put forward by Ivor Crewe. 'Voting and the Electorate', in *Developments in British Politics*, ed. P. Dunleavy et al. (1993). Changes in the social structure have weakened class and party loyalties, and 'on balance long-term structural changes in the British electorate are helping the Conservatives and hurting Labour.'

- The contraction of the traditional Labour's natural vote. working class has diminished 'The rapid spread of home-ownership, the migration from North to South and from inner city to suburb, and the expansion of non-union private sector employment have undermined working-class loyalty to the Labour Party.' Between 1964 and 1987 the professional and managerial class grew from 19% to 29%.

- Between 1951 and 1990 home-ownership more than doubled (from 31% to 66% of the electorate) and by 1987 a majority of working-class voters (56%) owned their own homes. 'Class has diminished, without disappearing, as a basis for party choice.'

- Voters have become less partisan. In the mid-1980s only a fifth of the electorate were self-declared 'very strong' identifiers with a particular party (compared with nearly half in the 1960s). The vote is more volatile – in a typical election nearly 20% of voters (almost 13 million) switch parties. The numbers of party loyalists have declined, Crewe argues that 'the best prospect for a Labour victory is the relapse of the economy into deep recession...'

- Critics see Crewe as overstating the decline of class and understating the autonomy of politics. Labour Party defeats in 1979, 1983, 1987, 1992 may have been the result of the party's moribund ideology and poor leadership rather than inevitable sociological trends. Parties can lose, and regain, credibility with voters. When Labour won the General Election of May 1997 the economy was – contrary to Crewe's prediction – far from being in 'deep recession'.

Ivor Crewe is a leading theorist on voting behaviour.

11.7 The Interactionist Model

- This was first put forward by Anthony Heath, Roger Jowell and John Curtice, *How Britain Votes* (1985). A key theme is that class has not withered away. However, the shape of the class structure has changed.

- The manual working class has contracted, the middle class has expanded, and the liberal wing of the middle class (public sector professionals) has provided fertile support for the Liberal Democrats. Although **absolute class voting** for the Labour

Party declined from 1964 to 1983 Heath et al. claim that **relative class voting** within the working class did not change. The same proportion of rank-and-file manual workers continued to vote Labour even though the total number of votes cast for Labour fell. Class dealignment was not taking place. The **odds ratio** — the odds of a member of the salariat (professionals and managers) voting Conservative divided by the odds of a working-class individual voting Labour — remained the same.

- The interactionist theory sees voting as a product of two factors:
  1 the class and social structure,
  2 the impact of political parties. Voting cannot simply be explained by sociological determinism.' It is also influenced by 'policies, record in office, putative (i.e. reputed) ability to implement a programme, unity of purpose, etc.'. Voting has to be understood in terms of the interaction between an individual's social situation and his / her perception of the political parties.

- Critics have questioned the analysis of the class structure used in *How Britain Votes*. Technicians, foremen, and the self-employed are not counted as 'working class'. In fact, Heath et al's working class only amounts to 34% of the working population. It is hardly surprising that this 'proletarian core' of the working class remains solidly pro-Labour in its voting with its relative class voting unchanged. Heath et al. vigorously reject the class dealignment thesis, even though support for the Liberals has increased from 2.6% in 1951 to 17.2% in 1997. Such an increase in third party support seems to be at odds with the view that classes have not 'weakened in cohesion.'

> In recent years supporters of the Interactionist Model have been engaged in vigorous controversy with supporters of the Class Dealignment Model.

> Examiners will expect you to formulate your own position on theories of voting behaviour.

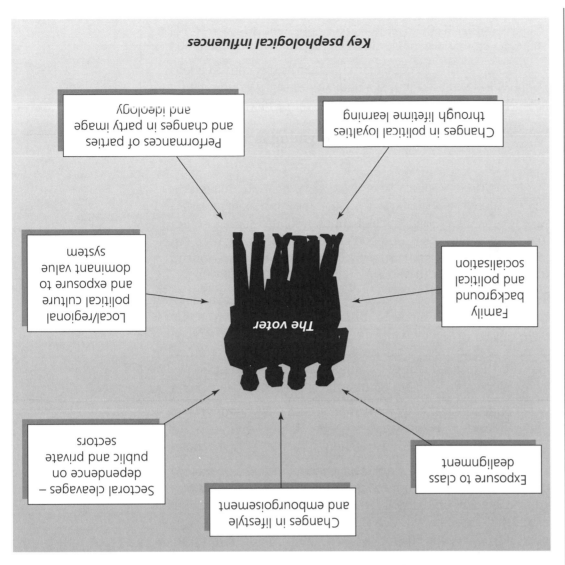

Key psephological influences

- Changes in political loyalties through lifetime learning
- Performances of parties and changes in party image and ideology
- Family background and political socialisation
- Local/regional political culture and exposure to dominant value system
- Exposure to class dealignment
- Changes in lifestyle and embourgeoisement
- Sectoral cleavages – dependence on public and private sectors

The voter

12 | The 1997 General Election

- The Labour Party polled 13,516,632 votes (44.3% of vote) with 418 MPs elected.
- The Conservative Party polled 9,592,999 votes (31.5% of vote) with 165 MPs elected.
- The Liberal Democrats polled 5,242,894 votes (17.2% of vote) with 46 MPs elected.
- Welsh / Scottish Nationalists polled 782,570 votes (2.6% of vote) with 10 MPs elected.
- Total number of votes was 31,248,597; 659 MPs were elected; turnout was 71.5%.

  (Key source: John Curtice, 'Anatomy of a Non-Landslide', *Politics Review*, September 1997).

- Election turnout was the lowest since 1935. It was down 6.2% on 1992, and was lowest in inner city poor areas.
- The 179 seat majority was the largest since 1935.
- 120 women MPs were elected – the largest ever. (101 are Labour MPs.)
- The overall swing to Labour was 10.3% across Britain. (The previous largest was 12.5% in 1945.) But Labour's share of the vote was lower than Labour achieved at any election between 1945 and 1966. Only three in ten of those eligible to vote voted for a Labour candidate.
- Note: there have been only three elections this century (1900, 1931, and 1935) when a party has polled over 50% of the vote.
- The number of votes cast for Labour was the highest since 1951. (In 1951 Labour gained more votes than the Conservative Party but lost the election. In February 1974 the Conservative Party gained more votes than the Labour Party, but lost the election.)
- The electoral system worked against the Conservative Party. Votes for the Conservatives were spread across constituencies rather than being concentrated. Thus the Conservatives gained 17.5% of the vote in Scotland but did not win a single seat. The Conservatives gained 19% of the vote in Wales but did not win a single seat. The Liberal Democrats gained 13% of the votes in Scotland and gained ten seats. Plaid Cymru gained 9.9% of the vote in Wales and won four seats.
- In terms of seats in the Commons the Conservative Party is left 'with a very narrow geographical representation. Of the 165 constituencies which elected Conservative MPs, only 40 are in very or mainly urban areas and only 45 are situated outside the four southern regions', David Denver, 'The 1997 General Election Results: Lessons for Teachers', *Talking Politics*, Autumn 1997.
- Sinn Fein gained 16.1% of the Northern Ireland vote (an increase of 6% on 1992).
- The Referendum Party (financed by the late Sir James Goldsmith) had 547 candidates and won 2.7% of the votes.
- There were considerable regional variations in voting, e.g. the increase in Labour's share of the vote was 12.5% in London but only 6.6% in Scotland.
- There was an increase in tactical voting. As a result the Liberal Democrats lost votes but gained seats.
- 259 new MPs won seats – more than in any post-war election. The average age of Labour and Conservative MPs is 49.8 (in 1996 it was 55).
- Social class continued to influence voting behaviour. 42% of the AB (professional and managerial) class voted Conservative, while 31% voted Labour. 61% of the DE (semi- and unskilled manual working class) voted Labour, while 21% voted Conservative. Support for the Liberal Democrats was highest amongst ABs (21%) and lowest amongst DEs (13%).

John Curtice refers to the election as a 'non-landslide' – do you agree?

Note the influence of class, gender, age, and ethnicity on voting.

- The gender gap disappeared. (In 1992 women were more likely to vote Conservative.)
- Age continued to be related to voting behaviour. 57% of 18–29 year olds voted Labour and 22% voted Conservative. 44% of 65 year olds and over voted Conservative compared with 34% who voted Labour.
- Ethnicity continued to influence voting behaviour. Only 8% of black voters, and 25% of Asian voters, intended to vote Conservative compared with 86% and 70% respectively who intended to vote Labour. However, turn-out was lowest amongst members of ethnic minorities, *Politics Pal* 1998.

13 | Checklist of key terms

Zero-sum concept of power   Influence   Authority   Globalisation   Hidden dimension of power   Manufactured risk   Separation of powers   Polyarchal democracy   Elite pluralism   Law of Anticipated Reactions   The Three Cs   Iron law of oligarchy   The Establishment   Totalitarianism   The New Class   Protective and Promotional groups   Insider and Outsider groups   NSMs and OSMs   Direct democracy   Indirect democracy   Psephology   Political socialisation   Expressive voting   Instrumental voting   Absolute class voting   Relative class voting

14 | Further reading

Kirby, M. (1995) *Investigating Political Sociology*, London, Collins Educational.

Mclean, I. (ed.) (1996) *The Concise Oxford Dictionary of Politics*, Oxford, Oxford University Press.

Roberts, G. and Edwards, A. (1991) *A New Dictionary of Political Analysis*, London, Edward Arnold.

Robins, L. 1998 *Politics Pal*, (available from L. Robins, 46 The Fairway, Oadby, Leicester LE2 2HJ).

Index